A Therapist's Guide to the

Personality Disorders:

THE MASTERSON APPROACH

A Handbook and Workbook

A THERAPIST'S GUIDE TO THE PERSONALITY DISORDERS:

THE MASTERSON APPROACH

A Handbook and Workbook

James F. Masterson, M.D.,

and

Anne R. Lieberman, L.C.S.W.,

Editors

Zeig, Tucker & Theisen, Inc.
Phoenix, Arizona

Library of Congress Cataloging-in-Publication Data

Masterson, James F.

   A therapist's guide to the personality disorders

      p. cm.

   ISBN 1-932462-09-0 (alk. paper)

   1. Personality disorders — Handbooks, manuals, etc. I. Title.

   RC554.M277 2003

   616.85'81—dc22   2003067246

© Copyright 2004

Zeig, Tucker, & Theisen, Inc.

Published by

Zeig, Tucker, & Theisen, Inc.

3614 North 24th Street

Phoenix, AZ 85014

Manufactured in the United States of America

10 9 8 7 6 5 4 3

Table of Contents

Contributors

Elinor Greenberg, Ph.D., former Faculty Associate, Masterson Institute, New York; private practice, New York

Arlene Hahn, C.S.W., Faculty Associate, Masterson Institute, New York; private practice, New York

Jerry S. Katz, C.S.W., Faculty Associate, Masterson Institute, New York; private practice, New York

Anne R. Lieberman, L.C.S.W., Faculty Associate, Masterson Institute, New York; Director of Clinical Services, Jewish Family and Children's Service of North Jersey; private practice, Ridgefield, N.J.

James F. Masterson, M.D., Founder and Director, Masterson Institute for Psychoanalytic Psychotherapy, New York and San Francisco. Professor Emeritus, Psychiatry, Weill Medical College of Cornell University

Candace Orcutt, Ph.D., Faculty Associate Emeritus, Masterson Institute, New York

Judith Pearson, Ph.D., Clinical Director, Masterson Institute, New York; private practice, New York

Steven K. Reed, Ph.D., Faculty Associate, Masterson Institute, Bellevue, Washington; private practice, Bellevue

Acknowledgments

This volume would not have been possible without the help of many dedicated people. Anne and I would particularly like to thank each of the authors for his or her diligence and effort in producing such excellent chapters. We would like to thank Carol Keeler, L.C.S.W., for the hours she spent composing the questions in the Workbook referring to Chapter 3. A Faculty Associate in New York, living in Florida, Carol composed a contribution that reflects the time and effort she always dedicates to her work. Much appreciation also goes to Angela Matthews, Psy.D., Masterson Institute Associate, for her thoughtful comments after reading the manuscript.

As with any manuscript, we all relied heavily on the computer. Anne and I are particularly grateful in this endeavor to Anne's three sons: David, for organizing the Workbook and translating e-mail documents into a format that Anne's computer could read; Michael, for tirelessly printing and correcting the manuscript while maintaining his sense of humor; and Jeremy, not yet in college, for his availability and willingness to help with all those annoying little details.

A special thanks to Nancy Scanlan for typing several chapters and for her struggles to make her computer communicate with Anne's.

Finally, a large note of appreciation to Suzi Tucker, our editor at Zeig, Tucker & Theisen, for her fine job of copy-editing.

James F. Masterson, M.D.
Anne R. Lieberman, L.C.S.W.

Introduction

Designed to serve as an introduction to the fundamental concepts, theories, and treatment approaches of James F. Masterson, M.D., this book is divided into two parts: a presentation of the body of his work, and an accompanying Workbook, in the form of a questionnaire, that will enable the practitioner to apply the skills he or she has studied. The combination of the two formats provides both a clear and a concise summary of Dr. Masterson's groundbreaking work and an unusual and intriguing way to enhance the learning process for the reader.

The body of the work is the subject of Dr. Masterson's 14 previous books and numerous articles. Read chronologically, these books illustrate the evolution of his theories of the Disorders of the Self (personality disorders), from their theoretical underpinnings to a treatment approach tailored to the specific needs of each disorder. Starting with his innovative work with the Borderline adolescent, moving on to the Borderline adult, and then to the Narcissistic and Schizoid Personality Disorders, his work has been a living thing, incorporating new developmental research, new research into the neurobiology of the brain, and new treatment approaches.

However, owing to their evolutionary nature, nowhere is there one source to which a therapist can go to gain an understanding of the basic tenets of the theories and clinical contributions. This book, written by members of the current faculty of the Masterson Institute, and by Dr. Masterson himself, aims to address this gap, providing the reader with a clear summary of the pertinent developmental theory and the evolution of the Masterson Approach; a definition of the fundamental concepts; a discussion of differential diagnosis; the etiology and treatment of the Borderline, Narcissistic, and Schizoid Disorders; the role of trauma and Posttraumatic Stress Disorder; and countertransference. It will not discuss in great detail all the complications and nuances of the work — the reader is directed to Dr. Masterson's earlier books for more in-depth material — but rather, its purpose is to simplify, clarify, and integrate.

The reader will be able to take from this book a theoretical understanding of the Disorders of the Self and will gain new skills to address two of the crucial tasks in the psychotherapy of these disorders. The therapist will understand, and be able to convert, transference acting out to transference and therapeutic alliance. He or she will also be able to identify the working-through stage and learn how to manage it so that the patient is able to stay in treatment and work through the painful affects against which he or she has been defending.

The companion to the text, the Workbook, utilizes a multiple-choice format designed to enhance learning in a variety of ways. Going over the questions is an educational process in itself, since it serves to emphasize the important points in each chapter, while underscoring aspects the reader might not otherwise have picked up. The questions vary from theory to practice, and often utilize examples of diagnostic considerations, interventions, patient responses, and follow-up therapist interventions. These exercises then enable the therapist to put into practice, to try out, the material presented in the first part of the book. He or she thus will learn how to differentiate among a confrontation, a mirroring interpretation of narcissistic vulnerability, and an interpretation of the Schizoid dilemma, and will learn when and where such interventions are appropriate in moving the treatment ahead. Once the reader has completed the questionnaire, he or she will have taken important steps in mastering material that has been demonstrated countless times to change the course of how he or she practices the art of psychotherapy. Ultimately, we hope that this step will be the first in a journey that will enhance both understanding and practice.

Anne R. Lieberman, L.C.S.W.

1

EVOLUTION OF THE MASTERSON APPROACH

James F. Masterson, M.D.

The product of many years of scientific inquiry, what has been termed the Masterson Approach first found expression through my own clinical work and research, and then, after many years of training, through the work of my associates in New York and California. It has led to two postgraduate training institutes (New York and San Francisco), as well as a nationwide society. Through a unified view of the growth of self and object relations, the Masterson Approach provides a unique window of observation on all the clinical vicissitudes of the Developmental Disorders of the Self.

The Masterson Approach evolved from constantly observing, empathizing, and speculating while clinically responding to the problems of adolescents and adults. It also required the integration of newly emerging psychoanalytic and neurobiologic theories of the development of object relations and the self with child-observation research that put these theories to the test of comparison with actual parent–child interaction.

A dynamic theoretical and clinical psychotherapeutic approach emerged that, I believe, has two major advantages: (1) it integrates developmental theory, attachment theory, object relations theory, and neurobiologic brain research theory with a psychology of the self, and (2) it provides its own self-corrective tools. It allows the formation of clinical hypotheses whose validity can then be tested in the clinical arena. Beyond that, it both widens and deepens the practitioner's area of observation and reflection, immersing one still deeper in the clinical endeavor, and equipping one to explore these complex subterranean themes with confidence and optimism.

Consideration of how the Masterson Approach developed can offer a deeper understanding of it. The pathway to the Masterson Approach can be divided into six stages, each of which had a central preoccupation, which was expressed in clinical research and resulted in a book. There was a progressive development of the point of view in each stage, each making its own contribution to the final perspective presented here as the Masterson Approach.

STAGE 1:
PSYCHIATRIC DILEMMA OF ADOLESCENCE (1956–1968)

During my residency, I began to notice at case conferences that whenever an adolescent was presented, someone was certain to point out that one had to be careful about diagnosis because "he or she may well grow out of it." I checked the literature for research on adolescents who had "grown out of it," and found next to nothing. Thus began a central preoccupation about "what happens" that was to dominate my professional life for 20 years and would involve three follow-up studies. During my last year as a resident and a postgraduate year as chief resident, I finished and published a follow-up study based on my research project on what happens to hospitalized adolescents. In short, they did not grow out of it.

At the same time, dissatisfied with the methodological limitations of a retrospective inpatient follow-up study, I wanted to do a prospective outpatient study that would eliminate as many of those methodological loopholes as possible. What I did not realize at the time was that I would be involved in a project from which it would take me 12 years (from 1956 to 1968) to extricate myself.

The size and the momentum of the research accelerated like a snowball rolling downhill. I now began to wonder if my reach had exceeded my grasp. It became necessary to drop my half-time clinical duties in order to find time for the research.

At this time, psychiatrists were starting to feel that their research methodology was inadequate as compared with that of the physical sciences. Thus, the social scientists came to the fore with their so-called objective research methodology focusing on such matters as defining variables, validity, reliability, and statistical analyses.

I came under the influence at that time of an extraordinarily talented social psychiatrist researcher, Alex Leighton, M.D., who was engaged in the now well-known Sterling County and Midtown Mental Health studies of the prevalence of psychiatric illness in the general population. He made his methodology and his statisticians available to us as consultants.

I grew conflicted, however, about the differences between the social science methodological point of view and the clinical point of view, which emphasizes the importance of considering all variables at one time and sees clinical judgment as the only final instrument of observation and decision. I would spend three hours a day at the clinic trying to redefine methodology — for example, conducting reliability studies or considering various statistical approaches to clinical material — and then go to an analytic session that would repeatedly demonstrate how often these activities did not seem relevant enough to the clinical material. After much struggle, I finally resolved the conflict in favor of the clinical point of view.

The findings of this project were published in a 1967 book entitled *The Psychiatric Dilemma of Adolescence*. We found that the adolescent did not "grow out of it." Five years after evaluation, more than 50% of the adolescents were severely impaired. At that time, we called the impairments personality disorders rather than borderline conditions, and we found on review of the treatment records that if the patients and their parents were treated once a week over the course of a year, their symptoms (such as anxiety, depression, and acting out) did indeed diminish. But what was giving them so much trouble five years later, their pathological character traits, had not been touched upon in the treatment at all.

I began to ponder how to pursue further the questions the study had raised. What were these pathological character traits? Where did they come from? How could we identify them, and how could we devise better methods of treatment? As I was considering these issues, I was invited to take charge of the adolescent inpatients at the Payne Whitney Clinic, who, in the past six months, had kicked out 50 door panels.

This was a serendipitous opportunity to pursue these questions in an inpatient setting over the long term, where we would have a chance carefully to monitor and correlate the interviews with the adolescents' behavior.

STAGE II:
TREATMENT OF THE BORDERLINE ADOLESCENT —
A DEVELOPMENTAL APPROACH (1968–1974)

At Payne Whitney, I designed a research unit for the intensive psychoanalytic psychotherapy of personality disorders in adolescents. Those next six years were extraordinarily fruitful for the development of my own thinking and, in retrospect, provided the bedrock of what later became the Masterson Approach.

The adolescents who were admitted had behavioral difficulties such as truancy, drug use, and other forms of socially unacceptable behavior. The principal clinical symptom was acting out. In order for the unit to survive, we realized that we had to find a means to set limits to this acting out. Having to deal with acting-out adolescents in a structured setting presented an absolutely unparalleled opportunity to learn how to understand and manage this defense mechanism.

The adolescents were forever putting the residents', and often my own, "feet to the fire" to test our competence and trustworthiness. Successfully surviving these adolescents' "trials by fire" taught us the therapeutic management of acting out. Only after we had become professionals at setting limits in order to survive did we learn that our limit setting had a far more important and profound psychodynamic effect. We saw the adolescents become depressed as they controlled their behavior, which provided the first important link between affect and defense.

It was now clear to us that the acting out was a defense against depression. However, the source of the depression remained unclear. We speculated that it might have to do with adolescent conflicts over emancipation. In trying to puzzle it out, I had exhausted all known resources, including the writings of Anna Freud (1958), Peter Blos (1962), E. H. Erikson (1956), and P. Greenacre (1960). The breakthrough in understanding the sources of the depression came while I was browsing through journals in the library and ran across an article by Margaret Mahler (1968) on her study of psychotic children entitled "Autism and Symbiosis: Two Disturbances in the Sense of Entity and Identity." This article led me to investigate further her reports of her child-observation studies of the development of the normal self through the stages of separation–individuation.

Mahler's work resonated with my own, and I jumped like a bloodhound on the track she outlined, following her work closely. At the same time that I was studying her work, our depressed adolescents began talking not about conflicts with their parents in the present or in the here and now, but about earlier and earlier separation experiences, and, finally, about their mothers' inability to acknowledge their emerging selves.

It dawned on me that again, serendipitously, I was in the midst of two complementary research experiments. In other words, Mahler's work educated me about the early development of the normal self, while my own adolescent patients were describing and demonstrating dramatically the failures of that normal process, the developmental arrest of the self of the Borderline Personality Disorder.

I put the two together, which led to the view that the Borderline Personality Disorder was a developmental problem — a failure in separation–individuation or in the development of the self.

This opened for me the doors to some of the mysteries of the Borderline Personality Disorder: the concept of maternal unavailability for acknowledgment of the self, the resultant abandonment depression, and the developmental arrest of the ego. It also led to an emphasis on a therapeutic technique — confrontation — that was integrated into the design of a treatment to deal with this developmental failure: confrontation of the adolescent's defenses against his or her abandonment depression led to the working through of the depression, which attenuated or removed the anchor from the developing, activating self and allowed it to resume its development.

These findings were published in a book entitled *Treatment of the Borderline Adolescent: A Developmental Approach* (Masterson, 1972). This book, in retrospect, must have been ahead of its time, as its appearance was greeted with thundering silence. I felt as if it had been dropped down a bottomless well. It was only after a second book,

The Psychotherapy of the Borderline Adult (Masterson, 1976), was published that the first attracted considerable attention.

STAGE III: 1974–1983

(1) *THE PSYCHOTHERAPY OF THE BORDERLINE ADULT —*
A DEVELOPMENTAL OBJECT RELATIONS APPROACH (1976);
(2) *FROM BORDERLINE ADOLESCENT TO FUNCTIONING ADULT —*
THE TEST OF TIME (1980);
(3) *THE NARCISSISTIC AND BORDERLINE DISORDERS —*
THE DEVELOPMENTAL APPROACH (1981);
(4) *COUNTERTRANSFERENCE AND*
PSYCHOTHERAPEUTIC TECHNIQUE (1983)

A key question remained: What was the link between maternal libidinal unavailability and developmental arrest? Object relations theory supplied the link that I had been looking for, and was an enormous catalyst to my own thoughts about the role of maternal acknowledgment in the development of the self and intrapsychic structure.

During part of this time, I had corresponded with Donald Rinsley, M.D., in what, in retrospect, seems to have been an unusual congruence of minds. I taught him about normal separation–individuation theory and the role of maternal libidinal unavailability in the Borderline Personality Disorder, and he taught me the finer points of object relations theory.

After the book on Borderline adolescents was published, I was scheduled to present a paper on the treatment of the Borderline adolescent at a symposium in Philadelphia honoring Margaret Mahler, M.D. Instead, I presented another paper on which I was working: integrating object relations theory with separation–individuation developmental theory. In this paper, I combined four ideas: (1) a developmental point of view about separation–individuation and maternal libidinal availability and acknowledgment; (2) object relations theory of the development of intrapsychic structure; (3) a very early paper by Freud on the two principles of mental functioning; and (4) my own clinical observation that as Borderline adolescents improved and became more adaptive, that is, as they separated and individuated, they felt worse, not better; in other words, they became more depressed. These four ideas were combined in a paper entitled, "The Maternal Role in the Genesis and Psychic Structure of the Borderline Personality Disorder." On the day that I presented the paper, I felt confident that I had made a breakthrough, at least for myself, and that a whole new perceptual world lay before me. I realized also that I would have to move out of adolescent psychiatry and into the broader world of the psychoanalytic developmental object relations approach to the personality disorders. After giving the paper, I sent it to Dr. Rinsley, who responded with great enthusiasm, and suggested that he might be able to integrate it better with Fairbairn's views on object relations. I agreed, and he became coauthor.

I was already applying these new ideas to adults in my own private practice. This work with adults was presented in *Psychotherapy of the Borderline Adult: A Developmental Approach.* This book changed, crystallized, and consolidated my developmental object relations point of view concerning the Borderline, as well as my professional image, which broadened from that of an adolescent psychiatrist to one of a psychoanalytic psychiatrist with an interest in the developmental object relations approach to the personality disorders in adolescents and adults.

I sent the book on the adult to my publisher with some misgivings, knowing full well that the adolescent book had not yet done that well. The editor sent the book out for review, and several very, very long months later, called me in for what was the briefest and most depressing interview of my life.

He turned the book down, quoting his reviewer as saying, "People interested in development read Mahler and there is much written on the Borderline. There is no place for your book." I felt dismayed and despondent. I had anticipated trouble, but not so much of it. Nevertheless, my conviction about the value of the work itself was not in the least shaken.

Luckily, through the good offices of another publisher, I was referred to Brunner/Mazel, who accepted the book immediately. One hurdle accomplished, I now had to await the book's reception. While it was being prepared for publication, a good sign occurred: the book was accepted as a selection by most of the psychiatric book clubs. But my doubts remained. I could not help but remember the awful silence that had followed the publication of *Treatment of the Borderline Adolescent.*

A good sale of a book featured by a psychiatric book club is several thousand copies. Several months after the book was published (1976), I found a note that my secretary had left on my desk. It read simply: "Psychiatric Book Club — 13,000." I knew immediately that the comma had been misplaced and that the figure was 1,300, not 13,000. And that was not too bad. As I brought the error to my secretary's attention, she assured me I was wrong; she had checked carefully. The number was 13,000. I cannot adequately describe the feelings of both relief and fulfillment that flooded me at the realization that the identity crisis was over.

That book had, and continues to have, an extraordinary record. It opened a whole new and exciting world. I received letters from numerous therapists across the country describing how exactly it explained their problems with the treatment of the Borderline patient and how helpful it had been. I also received any number of similar letters from Borderline patients themselves. I was inundated with requests for lectures, which attracted enthusiastic and responsive audiences. Concurrently, I found that my own integration of this developmental object relations point of view had greatly expanded my grasp and perception of clinical problems, as well as my ability to manage them.

This development also helped me to leave Cornell, which had been my professional home ever since I became a psychiatrist. I set up my own organizations: the Masterson Group for the treatment of the personality disorders, and the Masterson Institute for Psychoanalytic Psychotherapy, a nonprofit organization for teaching and research. This decision expanded my teaching from one institution to many. The Masterson Group had its inaugural public conference in October 1977 at Hunter College in New York. The subject was the Borderline Personality Disorder. We had planned for several hundred people; over 2,000 showed up.

In 1976, Jacinta Lu Costello, who was finishing her Ph.D. studies at Smith College, called me to ask if I would allow her to do a follow-up study of the Borderline adolescents treated in our unit. I was astonished that she would think that I would turn over these "jewels" to anyone else, since I had long planned to do the follow-up myself. We ended up doing a joint follow-up study of the Borderline adolescents treated in our unit, which was published in 1980 as *From Borderline Adolescent to Functioning Adult: The Test of Time*. This study demonstrated the effectiveness of the treatment, an effectiveness that could be predicted by the degree to which the patients' treatment course followed the hypothetical model. I then extended the clinical application of the theory to two other books, *The Narcissistic and Borderline Disorders: An Integrated Developmental Approach* (1981) and *Countertransference and Psychotherapeutic Technique* (1983).

In these books, a developmental object relations approach to Narcissism and the Narcissistic Personality Disorder was spelled out, and the concept of the underlying etiology of the Borderline Personality Disorder was extended as follows: There are three inputs into etiology — nature, nurture, and fate — and the therapist must make a clinical decision as to how much each has contributed to the patient's disorder. Nature consists of organic problems or constitutional or genetic defects. Nurture refers to maternal libidinal unavailability for support of the emerging self, regardless of the cause. And fate refers to those accidents of life that can affect either track of the two-track separation–individuation process; that is, any event that diminishes the mother's libidinal availability or interferes with the child's individuation in the first three years of life.

STAGE IV: 1983–1988.

THE REAL SELF (1985) AND

THE SEARCH FOR THE REAL SELF (1988)

By 1983, with the publication of the countertransference book, I felt that my writing days might be over. However, I also felt that the developmental object relations theory as outlined still did not give adequate consideration to the self, and the concepts of the self offered by others seemed to lack something. In my work with patients, I found myself, without intention or plan, focusing more and more on a patient's self, to the point of spontaneously developing symbols (S) for when the patient was activating his or her real self in the session and (O) for his or her relationship with objects. I began thinking and talking more in terms of a real and defensive self as it became clearer in the clinical material. Only after I had been using this concept of the self in psychotherapy for several years did I finally decide that I had to think it through further, organize it, and write it up, if only to clarify it for myself and to get it out of my system. This material became *The Real Self: A Developmental Self and Object Relations Approach* (Masterson, 1985). A second publication, *The Search for the Real Self* (Masterson, 1988), described the Disorders of the Self and their treatment for a lay audience.

STAGE V: 1988–1996.
THE EMERGING SELF (1993) AND
DISORDERS OF THE SELF: NEW THERAPEUTIC HORIZONS (1995)

The fifth stage comprised both further clinical exploration of the theory and the development of educational programs.

Exploration of the Theory

The early part of this long period involved exploring further, and in more clinical depth and detail, the clinical ramifications of the Disorders of the Self triadic theory. This led to the publication of *The Emerging Self* (Masterson, 1993), which presented a detailed discussion of the diagnosis and treatment of the Closet Narcissistic Personality Disorder, one of the most commonly overlooked diagnoses among the Disorders of the Self.

In the latter part of this period, the theory was enhanced by the work of two members of our clinical faculty, Ralph Klein, M.D., and Candace Orcutt, Ph.D. Dr. Klein masterfully put together and updated and integrated the work of Fairbairn and Guntrip on the Schizoid Disorder of the Self with the Disorders of the Self theory, to bring a brand-new appreciation of how to diagnose and treat this disorder, and his work has proved to be a significant addition to the growing body of theory about its etiology and treatment. Dr. Orcutt immersed herself in work with patients with trauma and Posttraumatic Stress Disorder (PTSD), and was able to integrate her conclusions into the theory, making the point that the therapist must pay equal attention to the trauma, the PTSD, and the character traits. Their work was published in *Disorders of the Self: New Therapeutic Horizons* (Klein, 1995).

Education

In order to expand the accessibility of this ever-accumulating body of knowledge further, I undertook the training of a group of associates, who then became the core faculty of the Masterson Institute for Psychoanalytic Psychotherapy. The purpose of the Institute has been to provide a framework for postgraduate, part-time, three-year training programs, both in New York City (since 1986) and in San Francisco (since 1988). By 2002, these programs had trained approximately 100 therapists. Annual two-and-a-half-day conferences have been held successfully in both New York and San Francisco. The Society of the Masterson Institute was established for those interested in the Institute's work. A newsletter for Society members is published twice a year.

STAGE VI: 1995–2002

In 2000, I published *The Personality Disorders* (Masterson, 2000), which reveals how the theory has stood the test of time in the areas of diagnosis and treatment. In addition, it presents the detailed treatment of a patient with a Narcissistic defense against a neurosis.

At this point, the puzzle seemed close to completion, with only two pieces missing: (1) scientific studies corroborating the mother's influence on the development of the self, and (2) identification of the neuronal networks underlying the development of the self. In an unparalleled explosion of knowledge, which has come to fruition in the last two years, both questions have been answered, the former by studies on attachment theory and the latter by neurologic brain research.

Attachment Theory

John Bowlby (1969) designed a model of emotional development that was free of drive theory and based on observable behavior that could be scientifically validated rather than using observation to infer what was going on in the child's mind. This research opened the model to further scientific validation, unlike the other models. His attachment theory was put to the scientific test by Ainsworth and colleagues (1978), who, following Bowlby's theory, carried out a pioneering study of the organization of infant attachment patterns into secure (60% to 70% of American families) and insecure. The insecure were further divided into avoidant, resistant, and disoriented/disorganized. These patterns have been repeatedly described by many attachment researchers, particularly Main and Hesse (1990) and Sroufe and colleagues (1999), with studies of adult attachment. Main studied the relationship of parents' attachment styles to those of their children. These findings were applied clinically by Siegel (1999) and Fonagy (2001), who found that the mother's style of regulation of the child's affect in the first 18 months of life has a profound effect on the development of the child's self and self-regulation of affect. If the mother's style is healthy, then the child develops a secure sense of self; if it is pathologic, the child develops a pathologic sense of self. Follow-up studies by Sroufe et al. (1999) have demonstrated that the attachment style of the child that is identified at 18 months persists into adulthood. Beyond that, identification of the mother's attachment style predicts the attachment style of the child.

All this work, in a wondrous way, corroborates in great detail the clinical basis on which we have been working all these years.

Neurobiologic Brain Research

Neurobiologic brain research has opened the door to understanding the neurobiologic wiring that underlies the development of the self. The important contributions of Allan Schore (1994) were of profound help in leading me to understand these neurobiologic developments, and they form the basis of this section.

The right brain is the container and regulator of affect, and its development dominates the first 2 1/2 years of life. A center for the self develops in the right prefrontal cortex at the apex of the limbic system, which has extensive connections with the limbic system, the autonomic system, and the rest of the cortex. The center emerges under the mother's regulation of the child's affect. At birth, the cortex is small, but in the postnatal years, until about 18–24 months, it grows 2 1/2 times its size. The mother's modulatory function is essential for the growth of the self during this time. She is thus the major source of environmental stimulation, which mediates genetic differences and facilitates or inhibits the experience-dependent maturation of the child's developing neurologic structures.

The right brain expresses itself unconsciously through tone of voice, facial expression, and body posture, which enables the child to become an active co-creator of his or her development through the mechanism of projective identification.

Schore (1994), combining the findings of attachment theory with this neurobiologic brain research, makes the point that if the mother's attachment style is pathological, the neuronal wiring essential to the development of a secure self will not develop and the result will be an insecure self, as the result of an underlying wiring defect, which is expressed clinically as a Disorder of the Self.

This theory of the self now seems to bring the developmental self and object relations approach to a kind of fullness and completeness appropriate to the demands of the clinical material. At least, it is probably as full or complete as I can make it. It is this comprehensive perspective that is called the Masterson Approach.

It has been exciting to have been fortunate enough to be involved in the veritable explosion of knowledge that has taken place in this field in the last 30 years, to see the gaps being filled and the pieces of the puzzle beginning to fit together. I had worked with Borderline and Narcissistic patients for years without being able to help them enough with their struggles. Finally, to have the tools to do the job with many patients, as well as to teach others to do the job, to have mastered this task — to the limit of my ability — has provided my ultimate fulfillment and satisfaction in the work.

This volume takes the work into a seventh stage, its faithful transmission to others who can deepen and extend it. The authors presented here have all been trained by me, and all are actively engaged in teaching others through the Masterson Institute for Psychoanalytic Psychotherapy. In addition to the three-year, part-time postgraduate training programs in New York and San Francisco, study groups, individual super-vision, and conferences for therapists are offered throughout the United States and overseas.

2

THE SELF IN THE PERSONALITY DISORDERS:

AN INTEGRATION OF ATTACHMENT THEORY, NEUROBIOLOGIC BRAIN RESEARCH, AND DEVELOPMENTAL OBJECT RELATIONS THEORY

James F. Masterson, M.D.

THE SELF

The Self, a key concept in this approach, has its own development, its own capacities or functions, and its own pathology.

The term "self" has been used by so many theoreticians that it is necessary to define it as I use it. I will define it first clinically, then from an intrapsychic object relations perspective, and then I will describe its capacities and its relationship to the ego.

The development of the self will be described in more detail to integrate attachment theory, neurobiologic brain research, and object relations theory. Attachment theory describes how the mother's affect regulation function mediates the expression of genetic influences and provides a vital environmental support for the development and wiring of the neurons in the prefrontal orbital cortex that will become a center for the self, which will then regulate the individual's affect and affective relationships. It also illustrates how these affective interactions become integrated to form the intrapsychic structure of the self.

Neurobiologic brain research demonstrates the neuronal structures that underlie the self. Object relations theory integrates both attachment and neurobiology to show how the structures find psychological expression and how they must be dealt with in treatment.

THE REAL SELF: CLINICAL

Self-image consists of the image that an individual has of himself or herself at a particular time and in a particular situation. It consists of his or her body image and the mental representation of his or her state at that time. This image may be conscious or unconscious, realistic or distorted.

Self-representation, a more enduring schema than self-image, is constructed by the ego out of the multitude of realistic and distorted self-images that an individual has had at different times. It represents the person as he or she consciously and unconsciously perceives himself or herself, and may be dormant or active.

Supraordinate self-organization refers to the fact that subjective experience may be organized by multiple self-representations; the "I" of one experience not necessarily being the same as the "I" of another experience. This term is used for the organization and patterning of the various subordinate self-images and representations. It connects them, and provides a continuity between them and a sense of unity and wholeness. This is one of the capacities that is pathologically impaired in the personality disorders.

THE REAL SELF: AN
INTRAPSYCHIC OBJECT RELATIONS PERSPECTIVE

The real self consists of the sum total of the intrapsychic images of the self and its associated object-representations. The term "real" implies healthy, normal, with a very important conscious reality component, although there are inputs from both fantasy and the unconscious.

The real, healthy self has two functions: it provides an emotional vehicle for self-expression, and it also operates to maintain self-esteem through the mastery of reality tasks.

Why the term "real self" rather than Winnicott's term, the "true self"? Winnicott's pioneering effort occurred before modern developmental studies had been carried out and was based on Freud's idea that there are two parts of the self, the part based on instincts, which was "true," and the part related to the environment or external world, which was false. Developmental studies have shown that this was a false dichotomy, since the self internalizes and integrates the early interactions with the mother and the external world to form an essential part of the self, which is then also invested with both libidinal and aggressive drives.

The term "real self" draws a sharp contrast to the false self of the Disorders of the Self. The false sense of self is not based on reality, but on a fantasy, and it maintains self-esteem not by efforts to master reality, but by defending against painful affects.

The real self consists of both the subordinate self-representations and the over-riding supraordinate organization. This real self has its own development, its own capacities and functions, and its own psychopathology.

THE CAPACITIES OF THE SELF

Spontaneity — Aliveness of Affect: The capacity to experience affect deeply with liveliness, joy, vigor, excitement, and spontaneity.

Self-entitlement: From early experiences of mastery coupled with the parental acknowledgment and support of the emerging self, the sense builds up that the self is entitled to appropriate experience of mastery and pleasure, as well as the environmental input necessary to achieve these objectives. This sense, of course, is sorely deficient in the Borderline Disorder and pathologically inflated in the Narcissistic Disorder.

Self-activation, Assertion, and Support: The capacity to identify one's unique individual wishes and to use autonomous initiative and assertion to express them in reality and to support and defend them when under attack.

Acknowledgment of Self-activation and Maintenance of Self-esteem: To identify and acknowledge to oneself that one's self (in both senses of the term) has coped with an affective state and/or an environmental issue or interaction in a positive, adaptive manner. This acknowledgment is the vehicle for autonomously fueling adequate self-esteem.

Soothing of Painful Affects: The capacity autonomously to devise a means to limit, minimize, and soothe painful affects.

Continuity of Self: The recognition and acknowledgment through an effective supraordinate organization that the "I" of one experience is continuous over time and is related to the "I" of another experience.

Commitment: To commit the self to an objective or a relationship and to persevere to attain that goal despite obstacles.

Creativity: To use the self to change old, familiar patterns into new, unique, and different patterns.

Intimacy: The capacity to express the self fully in a close relationship with minimal anxiety about abandonment or engulfment.

Autonomy: The capacity to regulate the affect of the self, independently of the object.

THE SELF AND THE EGO

The self and the ego develop and function in parallel; for example, like two horses in tandem in the same harness. The self is the representational arm of the ego, and the ego is the executive arm of the self, although each is more than that. If the ego is arrested developmentally, the self will also be arrested developmentally.

Erik Erikson (1956) referred to the dual and inseparable nature of the self–ego as follows: "Ego identity refers to the ego's synthesizing power in the light of its central psychosocial function, self-identity, to integrate the individual's self role images. One speaks of self-identity rather than ego identity when referring to the I perceiving itself as continuous in time and uniform in substance."

The self, of course, is mostly preconscious and conscious; the ego, through its synthesizing functions, is mostly unconscious. The ego's synthesizing function does for the psyche what respiration and circulation do for the soma.

DEVELOPMENT OF THE SELF, ATTACHMENT THEORY, NEUROBIOLOGIC BRAIN RESEARCH, AND OBJECT RELATIONS THEORY

The understanding of the development of the self began with direct child-observation studies by psychoanalysts of normal child development in the first three years of life. It has been exponentially expanded in recent years by attachment theory, neurobiologic brain research, and object relations theory.

The developmental forces that spur growth and development of the self are:

1. Genetic and biological
2. Pleasure in the mastery of new functions
3. Pleasure in sensory and motor functions
4. Reinforcement of the caretaking object for support of the self

THE PSYCHOANALYTIC CHILD-OBSERVATION APPROACH

Mahler

Margaret Mahler studied what she called the normal separation–individuation process by direct observation of infants from 2 1/2 months of age to their 31st month to determine how a child achieves a separate sense of self while functioning in the presence of the mother, that is, an intrapsychic sense of separateness of self from the mother, an independent identity.

Inferences were made from observation of an infant's behavior as to the infant's intrapsychic life. The observational process was extensive, with participant observations once or twice per week for each mother–child pair (dual unity). There were also weekly interviews with the mother, once-or-twice-a-year interviews with the father, filming according to a chronological guideline, and home visits of approximately one to three hours every other month.

The children received developmental psychological tests at least four times: at 5, 10, 18, and 30 months, and, in addition, the toddlers had play sessions. The mothers had an initial psychological evaluation.

Mahler assumed from her years of work with infantile psychotic children that the normal child had to separate from a symbiotic relationship with the mother. She divided the stages of development of the self as follows:

- Autistic stage (0–2 months)
- Symbiotic stage (2–4 months)
- Separation–individuation stage (5–30 months)
- First subphase — differentiation and development of the body image (3–8 months)
- Second subphase — practicing (10–15 months)
- Third subphase — rapprochement (15–22 months)
- Fourth subphase — consolidation of individuation and the beginning of object constancy (22–30 months)

Stern

Daniel Stern (1985) draws conclusions regarding the child's intrapsychic state from observing the child's behavior. Stern's work thus must be viewed as an invention — a working hypothesis regarding the infant's subjective experience of his or her own social life. It is a report not only of his own work, but of that of many others, including developmental psychologists in the burgeoning field of infant research. However, the work by Stern and the others was based more on experiment than on simple observation. And they approached it with a greater inclination to study what went on rather than to prove a hypothesis.

The essential findings can be summarized as follows:

1. The infant is predesigned to be perceptually separate from birth, with a fully active perceptual apparatus that seeks to organize his or her affective experience with reality.
2. There is a very active dialog between infant and self-regulating object from the beginning. The infant is a co-creator of his or her own development.
3. There is no stimulus barrier, undifferentiated phase, or autistic or symbiotic phase.

4. Self and self-regulating object-representations mature in parallel from the beginning.

5. Orality is not the special vehicle for internalization. All perceptual modes participate in internalization.

6. Id and the pleasure principle do not precede ego and the reality principle; a simultaneous dialectic evolves from the beginning of life.

7. Basic domains of human connection evolve from the infant's active construction of representations of interactions with self-regulating others.

8. There are four senses of self: emergent, core, intersubjective, verbal.

9. Senses of self are the primary organizer; there are sensitive periods, but all exist throughout life. Such issues as dependency and autonomy are not phase-specific, but are life-course issues.

10. The sharing of interpersonal experience or mental states creates "attunements" crucial to the growth of the self.

11. Selective attunement potently shapes the development of the child's subjective and intrapsychic life, that is, the infant becomes the child of his or her particular mother.

The Stages of the Self

There are four senses of self, each one defining a different domain of self-experience and social relatedness. Each sense of self remains fully functioning throughout life.

- The Emerging Self — 0–2 months: The experience of the emerging organization, the connection of diverse sensor-motor learning experiences. The first concerns the body: its cohesive actions, inner feeling states, and memory.

- The Core Self — 2–6 months: The child's experience of his or her own agency, affectivity, self-coherence, and continuity in time, and a sense of the other as distinct and separate.

- The Intersubjective Self — 7–15 months: The discovery that one has a mind that can be shared with another's mind. A theory of separate minds: interpersonal action moves from overt action to the internal subjective states that lie behind the overt behaviors.

- The Verbal Self — 15–30 months: A new medium of exchange evolves with which to create shared meanings — language. The child can begin to construct a narrative of his or her own life, moving relatedness onto the impersonal, abstract level intrinsic to language and away from the personal, immediate level. The capacities emerge to be self-reflective, to objectify the self, and to engage in symbolic action, such as play.

Attachment Theory

Bowlby (see p. 9) turned to ethology theory to postulate that all infants possess a basic instinct of attachment to caretakers and adapt their interpersonal behaviors in ways that assure them of adequate caregiver availability and responsiveness.

Bowlby's turn away from the intrapsychic to the environmental and from psychoanalytic theory to ethology alienated his work from the mainstream of psychoanalytic thought for a considerable time. However, the objective, scientific base of his observations lent them to later scientific study, and these studies have brought his work back to the mainstream.

In 1970, Ainsworth, following Bowlby's theory, carried out a pioneering study of the organization of infant attachment patterns into secure (60%–70% American families) and insecure. The insecure were further divided into avoidant, resistant, and disoriented/disorganized. These patterns have been described repeatedly by many attachment researchers.

A second generation of researchers examined the attachment problems beyond the first year of children of mothers who were depressed, bipolar, alcoholic, or maltreating, and they found all three to be insecure attachment patterns:

- The avoidant. The mothers were covertly rejecting, the infant was not upset at separation and avoided the mother on her return.
- The resistant. This was a much smaller number. These mothers were more disengaged and less responsive and the children showed alternate clinging and resistance.
- The disorganized/disoriented. The mothers were bipolar or depressed, alcoholic or abusive, or neglectful. The infants were not able to develop any consistent strategy for organizing approach–avoidance behavior to deal with discomfort under stress, therefore, they are called disorganized/disoriented.

Schore and Neurobiologic Brain Research

An exciting and profoundly important more recent contribution to our understanding of the role of the mother in the development of the child's self comes not from the psychoanalytic study of children, such as those by Mahler, Stern, and Bowlby, but from the world of neurobiologic brain research as reported by A. N. Schore (1994), who integrates attachment theory with neurobiology.

Findings

In the first years of postnatal life, the brain grows 2 1/2 times its size at birth. This human brain growth spurt is at least five-sixths postnatal, and continues until about 18 to 24 months of age. During this postnatal period, those brain regions in which the most rapid growth takes place are most susceptible or sensitive to external stimulation. Late-maturing cortical areas that differentiate after subcortical brain-stem areas are particularly sensitive to postnatal influence. Higher cortical levels come to inhibit earlier developing lower subcortical levels.

Thus, the major part of the development of the axons, dendrites, and synaptic connections that underlie all behavior is known to take place in early and late infancy. The growth of dendrites and synapses is experience-sensitive and experience-dependent, but the exact nature of such experience is still only vaguely defined. However, it is clear that the primary caregiver is the most important source.

The maturation of the right prefrontal cortex (the neurologic center for the self) occurs in the last quarter of the first year of infancy, and makes wiring interconnections that are affected by environmental stimuli during the critical period, which then become firmer.

Schore's Theory

A center for the control of affect, motivation, and social functioning emerges in the first year of life in the right orbital prefrontal cortex (the self). This happens during a developmental stage that begins at the end of the first year and ends in the middle of the second year. This late-maturing higher cortical structure is situated at the apex of the limbic system, and its extensive cortical connections and hierarchical dominance over the lower subcortical limbic structures account for its preeminent role in socio-emotional functioning.

It has been found that the expression of genetic influences requires transactions with the environment during sensitive periods. Maternal behavior itself is thought to be an external environmental event that mediates genetic differences.

Schore (1994) suggests that the practicing stage, roughly between 10 and 18 months of age, is a critical period for the development of social emotional function. At the end of the first year, increased, and more efficient, attachment functioning between the mother and child is associated with the appearance of high levels of positive affect that characterize the early practicing period, roughly between 10 and 12 months of age. These events, in turn, directly influence the growth of connections between cortical and limbic structures in the infant's developing brain that are associated with attachment function. A significant change in dyadic affective transactions occurring in the late practicing period accounts for the further maturation of these structures. The intervals between 10 to 12 months and 16 to 18 months are critical periods for the final maturation of the system in the right prefrontal cortex that is essential to the regulation of affect over the rest of the life span.

At birth, the human is remarkably ill-equipped to cope with the variations and excitations of the environment. He or she is a subcortical creature that is in danger of going into shock through overreacting to powerful or unexpected stimuli because of the lack of a means for modulating behavior that is made possible by the development of cortical control. The role of the higher structures is played by the mother. She is the child's auxiliary cortex.

Of special importance are late dyadic transactions with the mother in which she regulates the infant's affective state in the short term, which leads to structural change over the long term. Secure attachment facilitates the transfer of regulatory capacities from caregiver to infant. It is the mother's external regulation of the infant's developing immature emotional systems during particular critical periods of brain differentiation that is the essential factor that influences the experience-dependent growth of brain areas prospectively involved in self-regulation. This growth takes place in stages, and at the end of each stage, a more complex structure is capable of a more complex regulatory function. The outcome of effective dyadic affect regulatory transactions is an integration and restructuring of the infant's developing socioemotional regulatory system.

The need for attachment is what motivates the child's behavior. The attachment relationship becomes the dyadic regulator of emotion. Right-brain to right-brain attachment transactions between mother and child through projective identifications are central to the maturation and wiring of the infant's right brain, particularly the right prefrontal cortex.

These affective attachment experiences of infancy are stored in the right brain (the neurologic container of emotion) in terms of self- and object-representations and their linking affects, and they become working models of attachment relationships (what we will later call the intrapsychic structure). Strategies are encoded to use these models for coping with stress. However, these strategies, and the intrapsychic structures from which they spring, remain hidden from awareness by implicit memory. The child (or patient) cannot access them without help. Object relations theory will illustrate how the intrapsychic structure of the self finds expression in behavior and how it must be dealt with clinically.

3

THE MASTERSON APPROACH: DEFINING THE TERMS

Elinor Greenberg, Ph.D.

This chapter will briefly elucidate the basic tenets of the Masterson Approach to the diagnosis and treatment of personality disorders, as background for the chapters that follow, which will be more detailed and more complete.

The Masterson Approach is defined as a developmental, self and object relations approach. *Developmental* refers to the factors that lead a person to develop a personality disorder (Disorder of the Self). These notions are informed by infant developmental research, particularly the work of Margaret Mahler and Daniel Stern, and also by recent research on how the human brain is prewired to be affected on the neuronal level by mother–child interactions. Of particular importance are the work of Allan Schore (1994) on the role of the mother in affect regulation of the infant, Daniel Siegel's work as set forth in *The Developing Mind* (Siegel, 1999), and the work on attachment theory by Bowlby (1969, 1988).

Three factors play a role in the development of a personality disorder: nature, nurture, and fate. *Nature* means the genetic endowment of the infant. Just as people differ in athletic ability, intelligence, and appearance, they also differ in their capacities to have an autonomous self. Some children thrive where others fail to survive. *Nurture* refers to the mother's capacity to identify and provide emotional support for the child's individuating self. This term includes such factors as affect regulation and attunement to the infant's emerging self. The third factor, *fate*, refers to factors beyond the family's control, such as illness, death, war, famine, or other emergencies, that interfere with the mother's capacity and availability to support separation and individuation, or with the infant's ability to evoke and make use of maternal supplies.

The Real Self and the False Self

The factors that cause individuals to develop a personality disorder, by definition impair their ability to develop and express their "real selves." The term *real self* means the person's capacity to identify his or her own individuative wishes, to express them in reality, and to defend them when under attack. The real self encompasses the spontaneous and creative aspects of the self-organization. By contrast, the term *false self* refers to the construction of a way of being in the world and of seeing oneself and others that is alien in important respects to the individual's real self, is primarily reactive to the other, and lacks spontaneity.

The false self is further split into two part self-representations. For example, two typical part self-representations for a person with a Borderline Personality Disorder are that of being the good, loved, and helpless child (the rewarding part self unit), or, conversely, that of the abandoned, bad child (the withdrawing part self unit).

The Intrapsychic Structure

The term *intrapsychic structure* means the brain-based summary that resulted from the individual's early experiences with important caregivers. This summary includes all of the individual's self- and object-representations and their associated affects. Once formed, the intrapsychic structure organizes the way in which individuals perceive themselves in relationship to others. Thus, early experiences with significant caregivers shape later experiences of self and other.

Object Relations

The term *object relations* refers to the internal representations of self and others with associated affects, and how these structures then influence relationships with one's self and with others. Because of failures in development, a significant difference between people with personality disorders and those without them is that people with personality disorders do not have whole object relations. That is, their internal representations of themselves and others are split into two part-units. Each part-unit has a very extreme, unrealistic, and one-sided view of the self (the part self-representation) and a very extreme, unrealistic, one-sided view of the other person (the part object-representation). These part views of self and other with their associated affects alternate in various ways, but are not integrated and, therefore, not whole.

The object relations units of each of the three major personality disorders (Borderline, Narcissistic, and Schizoid) can be illustrated diagrammatically as follows:

THE MASTERSON INSTITUTE

A pervasive pattern of instability of interpersonal relationships, self-image, and affects, and marked impulsivity beginning by early adulthood and present in a variety of contexts, as indicated by five (or more) of the following:

1. frantic efforts to avoid real or imagined abandonment
2. a pattern of unstable and intense interpersonal relationships characterized by alternating between extremes of idealization and devaluation
3. identity disturbance: markedly and persistently unstable self-image or sense of self
4. impulsivity in at least two areas that are potentially self-damaging
5. recurrent suidical behaviors, gestures or threats, or self-mutilating behavior
6. affective instability due to a marked reactivity of mood (e.g., intense episodic dysphoria, irritability, or anxiety usually lasting a few hours and only rarely more than a few days)
7. chronic feelings of emptiness
8. inappropriate, intense anger or difficulty controlling anger (e.g., frequent displays of temper, constant anger, recurrent physical fights)
9. transient, stress-related paranoid ideation or severe dissociative symptoms

SPLIT OBJECT RELATIONS UNIT OF THE BORDERLINE

Rewarding or Libidinal Part-Unit (RORU) | **Withdrawing or Aggressive Part-Unit (WORU)**

Part Object-Representation: | **Part Object-Representation:**

 a maternal part-object that offers approval of regressive and clinging behavior

 a maternal part-object that withdraws, is angry and critical of efforts toward separation–individuation

(center, vertical: SPLITTING DEFENSE)

AFFECT

feeling good	being fed
being taken care of	gratifying the wish for
being loved	reunion

AFFECT
Abandonment Depression

homicidal rage	hopelessness and helplessness
suicidal depression	emptiness and void
panic	guilt

Part Self Representation: | **Part Self Representation:**

 a part self-representation of being the good, passive child — unique and special/grandiose

 a part self-representation of being inadequate, bad, ugly, an insect, etc.

Developmental Arrest of the Ego:
Ego Defects — poor reality perception; frustration tolerance; impulse control; ego boundaries.
Primitive Ego Defense Mechanism — splitting; acting out; clinging, avoidance, denial; projection; projective identification.
Split Ego — reality ego plus pathological (or pleasure) ego.

THE MASTERSON INSTITUTE

Narcissistic Personality Disorder Diagnosis Criteria
DSM–IV

A pervasive pattern of grandiosity (in fantasy or behavior), need for admiration, and lack of empathy, beginning in early adulthood and present in a variety of contexts, as indicated by five (or more) of the following:

1. has a grandiose sense of self-importance (e.g., exaggerates achievements and talents, expects to be recognized as superior without commensurate achievements)
2. is preoccupied with fantasies of unlimited success, power, brilliance, beauty, or ideal love
3. believes that he or she is "special" and unique and can only be understood by, or should associate with, other special or high-status people (or institutions)
4. requires excessive admiration
5. has a sense of entitlement, i.e., unreasonable expectations or especially favorable treatment or automatic compliance with his or her expectations
6. is interpersonally exploitative, i.e., takes advantage of others to achieve his or her own ends
7. lacks empathy: is unwilling to recognize or identify wtih the feelings and needs of others
8. is often envious of others or believes that others are envious of him or her
9. shows arrogant, haughty behaviors or attitudes

SPLIT OBJECT RELATIONS UNIT OF THE NARCISSISTIC PERSONALITY DISORDER

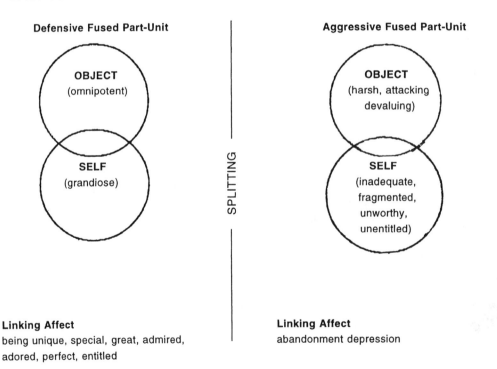

Defensive Fused Part-Unit

OBJECT
(omnipotent)

SELF
(grandiose)

SPLITTING

Aggressive Fused Part-Unit

OBJECT
(harsh, attacking devaluing)

SELF
(inadequate, fragmented, unworthy, unentitled)

Linking Affect
being unique, special, great, admired, adored, perfect, entitled

Linking Affect
abandonment depression

Ego Functions — poor reality perception; impulse control; frustration tolerance; ego boundaries.
Ego Defense Mechanism — splitting; avoidance; denial; acting out; clinging, projection; projective identification.

THE MASTERSON INSTITUTE

SCHIZOID PERSONALITY DISORDER DIAGNOSIS CRITERIA
DSM–IV

A. A pervasive pattern of detachment from social relationships and a restricted range of expression of emotions in interpersonal settings, beginning in early adulthood and present in a variety of contexts, as indicated by four (or more) of the following:

1. neither desires nor enjoys close relationships, including being part of a family
2. almost always chooses solitary activities
3. has little, if any, interest in having sexual experiences with another person
4. takes pleasure in few, if any, activities
5. lacks close friends or confidants other than first-degree relatives
6. appears indifferent to the praise or criticism of others
7. shows emotional coldness, detachment, or flattened affectivity

B. Does not occur exclusively during the course of Schizophrenia, a Mood Disorder with Psychotic Features, another Psychotic Disorder, or a Pervasive Developmental Disorder, and is not due to the direct physiological effects of a general medical condition.

SPLIT OBJECT RELATIONS UNIT OF THE SCHIZOID DISORDER OF THE SELF

Master Slave Part-Unit

Part Object-Representation:

 a maternal part-object that is manipulative, coercive, is the master and wants to use, not relate to

AFFECT

In jail, but connected, existence acknowledged, relief in not being alienated

Part Self Representation:

 a part self-representation of a dependent, a slave who provided a function for the object and is a victim

Sadistic Object — Self-in-Exile Part-Unit

Part Object-Representation:

 a maternal part-object that is sadistic, dangerous, devaluing depriving, abandoning

AFFECT
Abandonment Depression

Depression, rage, loneliness, fear of cosmic aloneness, depair

Part Self Representation:

 a part self-representation of being alienated, in exile, isolated but self-contained to self-reliant

(SPLITTING DEFENSE)

Developmental Arrest of the Ego:
Ego Defects — poor reality perception; frustration tolerance; impulse control; ego boundaries.
Primitive Ego Defense Mechanism — splitting; acting out; clinging, avoidance, denial; projection; projective identification, use of fantasy to substitute for real relationships and self-reliance.
Split Ego — reality ego plus pathological (or pleasure) ego.

As a result, people with Disorders of the Self are unable to see themselves and others realistically as whole, separate people, and therefore often misperceive the motives and emotions of others. This process leads them to misjudge situations and to act in ways that ultimately are not in their own best interests.

The Split Ego and Pathological Ego Alliances

Another reason why individuals with personality disorders have difficulty behaving in an adaptive and realistic way is that the ego is split into two parts: the reality ego and the pathological ego. This split is a result of an interruption in development, and is in accord with Freud's belief that, normally, the reality ego gradually develops from the pleasure ego. This development occurs only partially in the patient with a personality disorder, so that part of the ego continues to function in response to the pleasure principle. This part of the ego is called the pathological ego.

The pathological ego strives to avoid the painful affects of the abandonment depression. It supports the false self in denying reality and acting out instead of facing painful conflicts and activating the real self. For example, Ms. M, a patient with a Borderline Personality Disorder, had adult-onset diabetes and was supposed to eat carefully and to limit sweets. However, whenever she was on vacation, she would abandon her diet and eat rich desserts with every meal. She rationalized this by telling herself that anything she ate while on vacation did not count.

In this case, the pathological ego formed an alliance with the rewarding object relations unit (RORU), which took the form of being a little girl who was unable to resist temptation and take on adult responsibilities, such as regulating her food intake. If Ms. M had self-activated, kept her realistic health concerns in mind, and controlled her eating on vacation, she would have come into conflict with the part object-representation of her RORU. Then, instead of feeling love and approval as a reward for her regressive behavior, she would have experienced the affects of the withdrawing object relations unit (WORU). She would have felt like an unloved, abandoned little girl whose mother had become very angry and withdrawn whenever she acted grown up and capable. On an intrapsychic level, then, Ms. M had a conflict between the part of her that desired her internalized mother's approval and all the good feelings associated with that approval, and the part of her that wanted to act in a mature, healthy fashion. The pathological pleasure ego and its alliance with the RORU allowed her to keep the good feelings and to rationalize her dangerous behavior.

The Difference Between Neurosis and Personality Disorder

So many different things have been written about personality disorders that sometimes "personality disorder" seems to be simply a new term for what used to be called "neurosis." However, when one looks at the situation through the lens of intrapsychic structure, it becomes very clear. Individuals who have personality disorders have a split intrapsychic structure; those with a neurosis do not. The major problems for those with a neurosis develop after they already have successfully achieved whole object relations. As the capacity for whole object relations is a developmental achievement that usually occurs around the end of the first three years of life and continues to be consolidated throughout adolescence, this means that the problems we label "personality disorders" began before age 3 and interfered with the normal consolidation of whole object relations (Mahler, Pine, & Bergman, 1975).

Oedipal difficulties are an example of a neurotic conflict that occurs after the age of 3 and the development of whole object relations. As so much analytic writing has focused on the oedipal conflict, another common way of distinguishing disorders is to see the personality disorders as preoedipal.

In many cases, the Masterson Approach can give the person with a personality disorder a second chance to achieve whole object relations.

DIAGNOSIS

Diagnosis by Intrapsychic Structure

Diagnosing a Disorder of the Self is most effectively accomplished by mapping out the patient's intrapsychic structure, as opposed to looking only at behavior or symptoms (as the DSM-IV does, for example). People may behave similarly or have similar symptoms, but still respond optimally to very different therapeutic approaches. We assume that each of the three main categories of personality disorders (Borderline, Narcissistic, and Schizoid) has failed to achieve whole object relations, and that these disorders can be reliably differentiated from each other because each diagnosis has a distinctive intrapsychic structure.

With appropriate training and practice, one can infer intrapsychic structure fairly reliably from what the patients say and do in and out of session, their life histories, through attention to the style of transference acting out and to the therapist's own countertransferential responses.

Test of Diagnosis by Response to Treatment

The Masterson Approach to the psychotherapy of the Borderline, Narcissistic, and Schizoid Disorders is an integrated system in which the diagnosis and the choice of intervention arise from the therapist's hypothesis about the patient's intrapsychic structure and object relations. Each diagnosis receives different types of interventions that have been shown to work specifically to aid individuals with that diagnosis. The diagnosis is then reevaluated in light of the patient's response to the interventions. If the chosen interventions result in a lessening of defense, genuine self-exploration, a deepening of affect in session, and greater self-activation, then the diagnosis is assumed to be correct. If, however, the patient does not improve in these ways after a consistent systematic trial, the diagnosis is reevaluated, a different assumption is made about intrapsychic structure, and different interventions are chosen.

TRANSFERENCE VERSUS TRANSFERENCE ACTING OUT

Transference

Transference is based on whole object relations, which can be defined as the capacity to see the self and others as integrated and separate whole people, possessing both positive and negative traits. The patient who has whole object relations has also achieved object constancy and thus is able to maintain an affective tie to the therapist despite fluctuations in his or her feelings about the therapist (Mahler, Pine, & Bergman, 1975). Because the patient is capable of whole object relations, he or she is able to notice when his or her feelings about the therapist are unrealistic. He or she may say such things as, "I wonder why I keep reacting to you as if you were my mother." "Why do I feel so angry with you right now, when you are only trying to help me?" In other words, the patient can notice by himself or herself the difference between feelings and reality.

Transference Acting Out

Patients with Disorders of the Self do not have whole object relations and have not achieved object constancy. Instead of seeing the therapist and the therapeutic situation realistically, they project one of their part-object relations units onto the therapy, with its attendant part self- and part object-representations and associated affects. They then react, often becoming perhaps shocked, disappointed, withdrawn, clingy, or even angry when the therapist does not act in accordance with their projections.

What this pattern means is that these patients are reenacting over and over again, without conscious awareness, childhood interactions that have been intrapsychically encoded as a result of repeated interactions with parents and other important caregivers. Their intrapsychic structures limit their ability to see themselves and others realistically, to identify with and express their real selves, and to self-activate in pursuit of their real needs and wishes. As a result, their capacity for genuine intimacy is impaired. Because they are seeing life and its myriad possibilities in such constrained and constricted ways, patients who are transference acting out often misjudge situations badly and do not behave appropriately and constructively.

Another way of saying this is to say that the patient enters the therapist's office and unconsciously begins to act out the specific interaction that he or she had with a parent or parents. The patient projects the parent's image onto the therapist and assumes that the therapist feels and will act similarly to the parent. Without specific therapeutic interventions, the patient does not notice that this is not an appropriate response to what is actually occurring in the therapy session.

For example, Mr. D entered therapy and immediately started defending himself. His therapist had not attacked him, yet Mr. D acted as though he were being attacked. It was only after the therapist's interpretations brought this behavior to Mr. D's attention that Mr. D began to question his *a priori* assumption that the therapist was angry and disapproving.

The Abandonment Depression

Those with Disorders of the Self remain largely unaware of how much they are generalizing from past experiences with their parents. They have developed a defensive system that is designed to protect them from experiencing the painful feelings associated with their childhoods and with the lack of support that they experienced for their developing real selves. These underlying painful feelings make up the affects of the abandonment depression. The abandonment depression includes such difficult and painful feelings as suicidal depression, homicidal rage, panic, shame, guilt, hopelessness, helplessness, loneliness, and emptiness.

Analytic Neutrality

Analytic neutrality is a key component of the Masterson Approach. It does not mean that the therapist is cold or distant. Rather, it involves creating a therapeutic climate in which the therapist is attentive without engaging in caretaking behavior or being directive. The therapist keeps the focus on the patient, but, in general, allows the patient to lead without introducing personal material about the therapist or the therapist's emotional responses to the patient. The idea is to give patients a safe space in which they can explore their own thoughts and feelings without having to worry about anyone else's responses.

The Therapeutic Stance

The therapist also needs to take a clear, but mostly implicit, therapeutic stance that the patient is an adult who is expected to act appropriately in his or her own self-interest. Therefore, when the patient fails to act accordingly, an intervention is in order that highlights the inappropriateness of his or her defensive, regressive, or self-destructive behavior.

The Therapeutic Frame

The therapeutic stance is expressed by a clear therapeutic frame. The therapist maintains clear and consistent policies about such things as when payment is expected and how absences and lateness are handled. It is only against such a clear background that the patient's transference acting out becomes sufficiently visible that it can be used as the subject of an intervention. Thus, if a patient repeatedly comes late or "forgets" to pay on time, these are considered to be manifestations of transference acting out and are taken up in session.

Self-activation and the Disorders of the Self Triad

Self-activation refers to the awareness of, and expression of, aspects of the real self. Although self-activation ultimately leads to greater happiness and cohesion, patients first have to fight their way through immobilizing inner conflicts. Each time a patient self-activated as a child, a particular, specific, and generally unsupportive pattern of interaction took place with the parent. Over time, the awareness and expression of the unsupported aspects of the self came to be associated with anxiety, depression, guilt, and the other affects of the abandonment depression. In therapy, as patients begin to recognize, reclaim, and attempt to express these disowned parts of the self, they begin to feel the affects of the abandonment depression, which then lead to defense.

However, when the therapist intervenes successfully, patients begin to contain their defense and continue to self-activate. They then experience the affects of the abandonment depression that their transference acting out had kept out of awareness. Repetitive cycles of self-activation, abandonment depression, and defense, followed by therapeutic interventions, over time lead to resolution of the abandonment depression.

This three-part cycle, in which self-activation leads to the affects of the abandonment depression, which then leads to defense, is known as "the Disorders of the Self Triad." It grew out of the observation that therapeutic progress does not continue in a straight line. Awareness of the triad allows the therapist to understand, predict, and know how to handle a variety of difficult therapeutic situations.

STAGES OF THERAPY

The separation of therapy into discrete stages is an oversimplification for the sake of teaching. In reality, after an initial testing phase, most patients cycle through the triad over and over. Gradually, the defenses become increasingly ego-alien and the patient spends more and more time experiencing the affects of the abandonment depression. As patients do this, they gradually experience and work through their underlying pain by remembering past painful experiences, reexperiencing them, and understanding them in a new way. As each painful experience is worked through, energy previously used for defense is freed and the patient's real self emerges more and more. Over time, the patient begins to know and integrate the various aspects of his or her real self, as well as the good and bad aspects of the other. Ambivalence can be tolerated without splitting, leading to a capacity for whole object relations. At this point, the patient's creativity is freed up and he or she is able to experience and express his or her real self in a variety of ways.

Stage 1: Testing and Transference Acting Out

The patient enters therapy with his or her characteristic ways of transference acting out. These are ego-syntonic. That is to say, the patient accepts these behaviors as normal and natural. For example, a woman with a Borderline Personality Disorder of the Self saw nothing strange about impulsively picking up men in bars whenever she felt bad.

In the testing stage, while the patient is still largely transference acting out, there is little continuity between sessions. As the therapist consistently begins to intervene to interrupt the defense and bring it into awareness, the patient will test the seriousness of the therapist's resolve in various ways.

A frequent arena for this testing is around violations of the therapeutic frame, such as coming late to session, missing sessions, or forgetting to pay. If the therapist does not immediately take this up with the patient, the patient concludes that the therapist is not serious about the patient's behaving in an adult and constructive manner.

In this initial stage of therapy, most patients will reenact their repertoire of transference acting-out defenses, and consciously or unconsciously note whether or not the therapist colludes with them. If the therapist colludes, no real therapeutic progress will be made because all that is happening is that the patient's projections are being confirmed. It is, therefore, crucial to keep the frame in order to avoid collusion with the patient's defensive system.

The *therapeutic alliance* grows out of the testing phase, as the patient discovers that the therapist consistently intervenes in a way that limits the patient's regressive acting out, maintains analytic neutrality and the frame, supports the exploration and expression of his or her real self and is not drawn into one of the projected split object relations part-units. The patient and the therapist become a working team whose job it is to support the patient's exploration of his or her real self, self-activation, and appropriate constructive life choices.

Stage 2: Working Through

As Stage 1 gives way to Stage 2, there is the beginning of a real therapeutic alliance based on whole object relations. There is less and less need for the therapist to intervene to interrupt transference acting out because the patient is acting out less often and is likely to catch it himself or herself when he or she does. The patient is experiencing the abandonment depression and its associated memories and, as a result, is having insights about his or her life.

Because the working-through stage is such an intense emotional experience, the patient is frequently advised to come to treatment for more than one session a week.

With this frequency, the affects can be fully explored and contained in treatment so that they do not flood the patient.

Stage 3: Termination

The patient's growth as a separate, unique individual has resumed. The patient's real self has been freed up to continue its development and express itself creatively. The patient is now able to see himself or herself and others as whole, separate individuals, and thus is capable of real intimacy for the first time. At this point, the patient will experience a flowering of individuation, where real-self talents and capabilities will bloom. Because the process of termination reactivates separation stresses for both, the patient and the therapist will have to work through feelings that arise at this time.

4

THE MASTERSON APPROACH TO DIFFERENTIAL DIAGNOSIS

Judith Pearson, Ph.D.

WHY DIFFERENTIAL DIAGNOSIS?

A patient enters the consulting room and tells us about his or her life as he or she has experienced it. In its shortest definition, differential diagnosis is the way in which clinicians make sense of a patient's story, consolidating its disparate aspects under the rubric of a single coherent formulation.

In the Masterson Approach, diagnosis is of crucial importance, becoming the single best guide to the kind of treatment that will serve the patient best. If every patient were treated the same, differential diagnosis might be of academic interest, but it would hold very little clinical significance. To formulate a diagnosis according to the tenets of the Masterson Approach, one must have a basic knowledge of the theoretical premises on which the approach stands. The first section of this chapter will deal with salient features common to all Disorders of the Self. Following this, a brief description of the distinguishing characteristics of each of the disorders will be presented. Having built this framework, the elements that enter into the formulation of a diagnosis will be elucidated.

THE MASTERSON APPROACH VS. DSM:
STRUCTURE VS. SYMPTOM

Most clinicians begin the process of making a diagnosis by consulting the *Diagnostic and Statistical Manual of Mental Disorders* (DSM-IV) (1994). The DSM is helpful in explicating the behavioral correlates of psychopathology (the symptom picture). The Masterson Approach goes deeper by condensing psychodynamic, developmental, and structural issues, relying on an assessment of the patient's intrapsychic structure, including his or her internalized self- and object-representations, ego functioning, and ego defenses.

The Masterson Approach's focus on structure as opposed to symptom has led to a shift in diagnostic categories, subsuming the 11 personality disorders listed in DSM under four categories, while adding subtypes of the Borderline, Narcissistic, and Schizoid Disorders that are unacknowledged by the DSM. In accord with the Masterson classificatory system:

1. The *Borderline Disorder of the Self* subsumes the histrionic, dependent, passive-aggressive, and compulsive personality types and includes clinging and distancing subtypes.
2. For the *Narcissistic Disorder of the Self*, DSM's symptom picture is congruent only with the Exhibitionistic Narcissistic subtype. The Masterson Approach additionally includes Closet and Devaluing subtypes.
3. The *Antisocial Disorder* remains consistent with the DSM symptom picture, but in the Masterson Approach, reliance is placed on the emotionally detached nature of the patient's internalized object relations, rather than on the presenting symptoms.
4. The *Paranoid and Schizoid Disorders of the Self* subsume the Paranoid, Schizoid, Avoidant, and Schizotypal personalities under this rubric and add the Secret, Borderline Cluster, and Narcissistic Cluster subtypes to the Schizoid diagnosis.

These diagnostic entities rearrange themselves in this fashion because their classification no longer depends on the static and superficial aspect of symptom, but rather upon the enduring and dynamic characteristics of intrapsychic structure.

THE MASTERSON APPROACH TO
INTRAPSYCHIC STRUCTURE

The first notions of intrapsychic structure were set down by Freud as he delineated the topographic features of id, ego, and superego, and went on to say that all behavior, including symptoms, represented a compromise solution to the conflicts undergone by these agencies of the self as they struggled with each other and with reality. In this one-person psychology, attachment represented a vicissitude of libido whereby love was a by-product of need satisfaction.

With the advent of the British object relations school, however, attachment itself was elevated to the status of a primary drive — in fact, the primary drive — which acted as the dynamic organizer of the self, such that the self in affective interaction with the other constituted a relational unit whose aspects became internalized in the form of object relations units consisting of a self-representation, an object-representation, and a linking affect.

Like the British school, the Masterson Approach postulates that the drive for attachment is the primary motivational organizer of the self. The child's own temperament and the vicissitudes of fate, which arise during the formative preoedipal years, are major contributors to personality development. With regard to the former, it has been thought possible that children may have innate differences in their capacities for the work of separation and/or individuation. External events occurring during the crucial preoedipal period will also play a role. So, for example, a child rendered immobile by an accident or chronic illness may have more difficulty with these developmental processes. Similarly, a death in the family and the mother's natural mourning may make a mother less attuned to her child's needs during this critical period, or loss of a job by a father may create family strife that interferes with the child's growth and well-being. But the primary factor determining the intrapsychic structure of a child will still be held in the specific nature of the mother–child relationship. Where there is sufficient maternal libidinal investment in the child's growing self, normal development will occur. Where the mother's libidinal investment is insufficient, that is, where there is neglect, abuse, trauma, chronic misattunement, or persistent emotional pressure on a child to submit to a relational bargain primarily designed to serve the mother's psychological needs as opposed to the child's, a Disorder of the Self will result that will manifest itself as a stable diagnostic entity with its own structural characteristics.

DIAGNOSTIC FEATURES OF DISORDERS OF THE SELF

1. *Nonspecific ego weaknesses*, including poor reality testing, impaired insight and judgment, poor frustration tolerance, and poor impulse control. It is characteristic of all Disorders of the Self that the behests of the pleasure ego win out over the more sober perspectives of the reality ego.

2. *Primitive ego defenses*, such as idealization, projection, projective identification, denial, externalization, superego lacunae, and, most famously, splitting, are utilized. Since the genesis of Disorders of the Self occurs in the preoedipal period

before the advent of the capacity to integrate "good" and "bad" aspects of self and other into whole object-representations that encompass both, a signal feature of the disorders revolves around the presence of two unintegrated object relations units: the libidinal (good self, good object, good feeling) unit, and the aggressive (bad self, bad object, abandonment-depression feeling) unit. The formal feature of splitting exists in all the Disorders of the Self. The patient's diagnosis will be largely dependent on the specific content of these internalized representational units and the way in which they reflect his or her unique object relational history.

3. *Sacrifice of real-self activation to false-self compliance.* A significant feature of all Disorders of the Self is the presence of a false self developed in compliance with the needs of the object. The nature of the false self will be determined by the specific demands and impingements exerted by the object on the child's developing self, which stand in contradiction to the child's real-self needs and feelings. The self-disordered patient's false self will be evidenced by continuous stagnant repetitions of maladaptive, intrapsychically anchored patterns of object relations, as well as by impairments in the sense of self-identity, adaptive functioning, creativity, and self-expression.

4. *Abandonment depression and the central psychodynamic theme of the Disorders of the Self Triad.* Failure of the mother to provide libidinal supplies for the child's developing self will occasion what Dr. Masterson has characterized as the abandonment depression, a complex affective response with six components, including suicidal depression, homicidal rage, panic, emptiness and void, helplessness and hopelessness, and guilt. Once established, the existence of the abandonment depression will engender in the child a propensity for relinquishing all real-self feelings and activities that would reactivate these painful affects. In treatment, a central psychodynamic theme will occur whereby the patient's attempts to activate his or her real self will result in the experience of abandonment depression, and a consequent reinstitution of defense. The repetitive cycle whereby self-activation leads to the affects of the abandonment depression, and then to a remobilization of defense, is a stable, reliable diagnostic feature of the psychotherapy of the Disorders of the Self. Dr. Masterson refers to this characteristic pattern as the Disorders of the Self Triad.

5. *Transference acting out vs. transference.* The concept of transference as it was first described referred to the neurotic patient who had attained whole object relations, and so was able to view the analyst as a whole separate person with good and bad aspects, with whom a working alliance could be established that was centered on the task of defeating the patient's neurosis. Onto the screen of the working alliance was projected the transference, wherein the analyst was experienced as if he or she were like a parent or other significant person in the patient's life. For the self-disordered patient who lacks whole object relations,

there exists no "as if" quality in the transference. Instead, the therapist is experienced as being the parent in either his or her (usually her) good or bad dimension, and is then responded to accordingly. To emphasize this crucial clinical difference, Dr. Masterson retains the term *transference* when referring to the whole-self and object-based transferential responses of the neurotic, but indicates that the split-self and object-based transferential responses of self-disordered patients are more accurately defined by the term *transference acting out*.

For all Disorders of the Self, upper-level patients will largely tend toward transference acting out of the libidinal "good" internalized object relations unit, whereas lower-level patients will be more likely to engage in transference acting out of the aggressive "bad" internalized object relations unit.

DIFFERENTIATING THE DISORDERS

The characteristics delineated above represent diagnostic markers for all Self Disorders. The differences between disorders, that is, the unique intrapsychic elements that demarcate the diagnostic boundaries that both define and differentiate the Borderline, Narcissistic, and Schizoid Disorders of the Self, will be determined by the specific content of the patient's internalized object relational units, which, in turn, will be dictated by the relational dynamic imposed on the child during the child's preoedipal history. Thus, the nature of the disorder will depend on the specific characteristics of the mother's impingements on the child's developing self. The severity of the disorder (upper level, midlevel, or lower level) will be dependent on the intensity and pervasiveness of these impingements. In order better to understand the similarities and differences that exist among the disorders, the three diagrams first appearing in Chapter 3 (p. 25, and discussed in more detail in subsequent chapters) have been drawn that schematically represent the Borderline, Narcissistic, and Schizoid Disorders respectively.

THE BORDERLINE DISORDER OF THE SELF

According to the DSM-IV (1994), the Borderline Personality Disorder is defined as demonstrating at least five of the following characteristics: (1) impulsivity or unpredictability in at least two areas that are potentially self-damaging; (2) a pattern of unstable and intense interpersonal relationships; (3) inappropriate intense anger or lack of control of anger; (4) identity disturbance; (5) affective instability; (6) intolerance of being alone; (7) physically self-damaging acts; (8) chronic feelings of emptiness or

SPLIT OBJECT RELATIONS UNIT OF THE BORDERLINE

Rewarding or Libidinal Part-Unit (RORU) | **Withdrawing or Aggressive Part-Unit (WORU)**

Part Object-Representation:

 a maternal part-object that offers approval of regressive and clinging behavior

Part Object-Representation:

 a maternal part-object that withdraws, is angry and critical of efforts toward separation–individuation

SPLITTING DEFENSE

AFFECT

feeling good	being fed
being taken care of	gratifying the wish for
being loved	reunion

AFFECT
Abandonment Depression

homicidal rage	hopelessness and helplessness
suicidal depression	emptiness and void
panic	guilt

Part Self Representation:

 a part self-representation of being the good, passive child — unique and special/grandiose

Part Self Representation:

 a part self-representation of being inadequate, bad, ugly, an insect, etc.

Developmental Arrest of the Ego:

Ego Defects — poor reality perception; frustration tolerance; impulse control; ego boundaries.

Primitive Ego Defense Mechanism — splitting; acting out; clinging, avoidance, denial; projection; projective identification.

Split Ego — reality ego plus pathological (or pleasure) ego.

boredom. It is certainly true that most clinicians have encountered Borderline patients who fully demonstrate these behaviors. However, the diagnostic schema at the heart of the Masterson Approach also makes room for the many upper-level Borderline patients who do not meet the criteria expressed in the DSM. Therefore, rather than relying solely on these symptoms as a basis for diagnosis, we will turn to the more reliable diagnostic guidelines encompassed by intrapsychic structure.

The genesis of Borderline pathology is a consequence of maternal failure to provide sufficient and appropriate libidinal supplies for the child's twofold labor of separation, which consists of separating the internalized representation of self from the internalized representation of mother, and individuation, which consists of the child's capacity to bring to flower his or her own unique talents and abilities. Where the mother's attunement and resources are fully available to the child, the dual processes of separation and individuation will allow for the integration of good and bad aspects of self and object, creating an intrapsychic universe of whole object relations, adaptive ego functioning, and healthy self-identity.

Where, however, the mother's own psychological needs propel her to withdraw her supplies in response to her child's growing separation and autonomy, a condition is set for a developmental failure triggered by two patterns of mother–child interaction: maternal reward for failures associated with the tasks of separation–individuation, and maternal withdrawal for attempts at separation–individuation. These two repetitive patterns then become institutionalized as psychic structures in the form of the part self- and part object-representational units shown in the diagram of the Borderline Disorder of the Self (see p. 25). Thus, on the libidinal side of the splitting defense, the unit of attachment will consist of the rewarding object relations unit (RORU), which contains a part self-representation of being good, special, and compliant, with an associated part object-representation of a maternal object who offers approval for regressive and clinging behavior. The linking affect joining these representations is that of feeling good, being taken care of, and being loved. Separated from the rewarding unit by the splitting defense is the withdrawing object relations unit (WORU), consisting of a part self-representation of being inadequate, selfish, bad, and ugly, and a part object-representation of a maternal object who is angry, critical, withdrawing, and hostile in response to attempts at separation–individuation. The linking affect joining these two part representations is the abandonment depression.

Having reviewed the intrapsychic structure of the Borderline Disorder, the question remains as to how that structure manifests itself in behavior. In simplest terms, one could say that all the functioning of those with a Borderline Disorder of the Self is aimed at avoiding the feelings on the WORU side of the chart. That is, a Borderline patient's mission in life is to avoid the feelings of the abandonment depression and to keep the rewarding unit constantly activated. Because the rewarding unit operates in accord with the behests of the pleasure rather than the reality ego, reality concerns are sacrificed, so that the Borderline patient pays a high price for his or her pathology. This price is then denied.

In concrete terms, these dynamics imply the sacrifice of life challenges to regressive behavior as a way of warding off the affects of the abandonment depression. The capacity for healthy relationships will also be affected, as the individual with this disorder continues to act out projections and to rely on defensive patterns of clinging and distancing. In the treatment, transference acting out assumes the form of trying to coerce the therapist into resonating with these two intrapsychic units — the upper-level Borderline patients, prone to clinging, tending to locate their projections on the therapist more within the confines of the rewarding unit, with lower-level Borderline patients being more apt to demonstrate distancing patterns and negative projections consistent with the projection of the withdrawing unit.

As is true of all Self Disorders, the specific nature of the Borderline Disorder's pathology will be best served by a specific form of intervention, namely, confrontation, which is designed to interrupt these firmly entrenched defensive patterns and to offer the patient the libidinal push necessary to continue the work of separation–individuation. In making a differential diagnosis, the patient's positive response to confrontation, as evidenced by improvement in affect management, adaptive functioning, and object relations, along with the concomitant emergence of the affects of the abandonment depression in the treatment room, provides significant confirmation that a diagnosis of Borderline Disorder of the Self is accurate.

THE NARCISSISTIC DISORDER OF THE SELF

In depicting the clinical picture of the Narcissistic Disorder of the Self, we will again begin with the formulations arrived at in the DSM-IV, which sees the disorder as displaying the following features: (1) a grandiose sense of self-importance or uniqueness; (2) preoccupation with fantasies of unlimited success; (3) exhibitionistic need for constant attention and admiration; (4) characteristic responses to threats to self-esteem; and (5) characteristic disturbances in interpersonal relationships, such as feelings of entitlement, interpersonal exploitiveness, relationships that alternate between the extremes of overidealization and devaluation, and lack of empathy.

As was true of the Borderline Disorder, the DSM's description of the Narcissistic Disorder goes far, but not far enough, explicating a symptom picture that is pertinent only to what the Masterson Approach has defined as the Exhibitionistic or Grandiose subtype of Narcissistic Disorder. And it might be parenthetically noted here that any clinician who has encountered this personality in the consulting room rarely needs a handbook to arrive at a diagnosis. So again we will supplement the DSM symptom picture with the Masterson Approach's emphasis on developmental history and intrapsychic structure.

The attributes delineated by the DSM's description of the Narcissistic Disorder are pathological in an adult, but quite appropriate to a newly mobile toddler engaged in what one developmental theorist called "a love affair with the world." Full of a sense of just-won power, able to stand on his or her own two feet and explore a universe alive with sound and color and smell, the unquenchable delight and sense of grandiosity of this young toddler stand in sharp contrast to the depression and anxiety of the older, "terrible-two-ish" "rapprochement" child engaged in the work of separation–individuation. This difference is directly traceable to the fact that the younger "practicing" child is still in a state of intrapsychic fusion with a perceivedly omnipotent maternal object.

The mother's capacity to provide refueling and to meet the child's real achievements with appropriate mirroring provides the child with sufficient libidinal supplies to respond to normal frustrations with a modulation of his or her grandiosity. Tolerable levels of disappointment promote the recognition that the child and mother are not one, and one-mindedness is renounced as the internal work of separating intrapsychic self- and object-representations ushers in the next phase of development. Where the mother's pathology is such that she requires the child to resonate to her own narcissistic projections, mirroring will be unempathic and defective, leading to the preservation of unmodulated grandiosity as a way of defending the underlying, unsupported empty and fragmented real self.

These maladaptive relational patterns then become internalized as two fused part-object relations units (see diagram 2, pp. 26, 44): the grandiose part self/omnipotent part object unit, and the empty part self/aggressive part object unit.

A description of the libidinal grandiose/omnipotent fused unit consists of a grandiose part-self representation that has the characteristics of being superior, elite, and exhibitionistic fused with an omnipotent part object-representation that contains all power perfection and supplies. The linking affect is one of feeling perfect, powerful, special, and unique. This libidinal unit of attachment is separated by the splitting defense from the aggressive unit, which is composed of a part self-representation of being humiliated, attacked, fragmented, and empty, fused with a part object-representation that is harsh, attacking, critical, and punitive. The linking affect of this empty/aggressive unit is the abandonment depression.

As with the Borderline personality, the defensive or grandiose fused part unit forms an alliance with the pathological pleasure ego to ward off the affects of the abandonment depression. However, whereas the Borderline patient's abandonment depression is triggered by separation stress or attempts at individuative self-activation, the Narcissistic patient's abandonment depression is precipitated either by the pursuit of real self as opposed to narcissistic goals, or by the sense of the object's failure to provide narcissistic supplies in the form of idealizable omnipotence or perfect mirroring. The defensive response to narcissistic injury and its consequences — abandonment depression, narcissistic rage, and fragmentation — will be an attempt to reactivate the grandiose/omnipotent unit by avoiding, denying, or devaluing the offending object.

This depiction is most appropriate for the Exhibitionistic or Grandiose subtype of the Narcissistic Disorder, but the Masterson Approach has identified two other subtypes of the Narcissistic Disorder: the Closet Narcissistic Disorder and the Devaluing Narcissistic Disorder.

The Closet Narcissistic Disorder is so named because, unlike the Exhibitionistic Narcissistic personality, the Closet Narcissistic patient's goes underground. For whereas the Exhibitionistic Narcissistic patient's false self is structured around the need to obtain maternal mirroring by continuously living up to the mother's idealizing projections, the individual with a Closet Narcissistic Disorder must continuously avoid the mother's hostility, envy, and attack by mirroring the mother and denying his or her

SPLIT OBJECT RELATIONS UNIT OF THE NARCISSISTIC PERSONALITY DISORDER

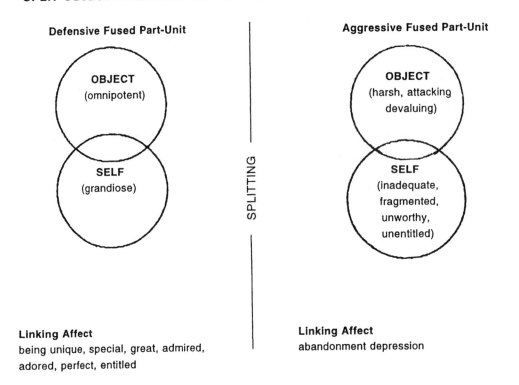

Defensive Fused Part-Unit

OBJECT
(omnipotent)

SELF
(grandiose)

SPLITTING

Aggressive Fused Part-Unit

OBJECT
(harsh, attacking
devaluing)

SELF
(inadequate,
fragmented,
unworthy,
unentitled)

Linking Affect
being unique, special, great, admired,
adored, perfect, entitled

Linking Affect
abandonment depression

Ego Functions — poor reality perception; impulse control; frustration tolerance; ego boundaries.
Ego Defense Mechanism — splitting; avoidance; denial; acting out; clinging, projection; projective
   identification.

own grandiose wishes. Narcissistic supplies are then derived by basking in the glow of the idealized other's reflected glory.

However, underlying the self-effacing façade of the Closet Narcissistic Disorder lies the pool of infantile grandiosity that could not be made manifest, and was, therefore, never modulated. So, despite their very different outward presentations, the Exhibitionistic and Closet Narcissistic Disorders are but two sides of the same structural coin.

The Devaluing Narcissistic Disorder is perhaps the easiest subtype to diagnose, and the hardest subtype to treat. The devaluing patient differs from his or her Narcissistic counterparts, the Exhibitionistic and the Closet individuals, in that these subtypes will primarily demonstrate the projection of early idealizing or mirroring patterns, with projection of the empty/aggressive part unit taking on a secondary role. In some patients, however, both core self structure and ego defenses are so primitive and fragile as to preclude the therapeutic mobilization of idealizing or mirroring patterns. The pervasive need to defend against internalized persecutory objects leads to reliance on rigid pathological defenses that serve the purpose of extruding and denying intolerable feeling. The ability to sustain activity in the external world that ensures the more successful Narcissistic individual some measure of supplies is, in these less capable patients, limited or damaged, as the observing ego and tolerance of delay or disappointment are easily breached, to be replaced by poor impulse control and a failure to tolerate and master anxiety. In treatment, the patient demonstrates a predominance of paranoid trends that infiltrate the therapy and create massive obstacles to the capacity to form a therapeutic alliance. Internalized representations of parental intrusion, abuse, neglect, and misattunement are continuously in play, so that these patients, who experience virtually continuous rupture of the grandiose defense, must rely instead on defensive projection of the aggressive part-unit.

Before closing our discussion of the Narcissistic Disorder, a word about treatment. Although confrontation can be seen as the best way to serve the psychological needs of the Borderline, this kind of intervention would only repel the injury-sensitive Narcissistic patient. Instead, the intervention most suited to the intrapsychic world of the Narcissistic patient consists of what the Masterson Approach defines as a Mirroring Interpretation of Narcissistic Vulnerability that addresses the pain of the patient's real self in response to situations of narcissistic injury, and the defense used to ward off that pain. The patient's responses to these interventions will serve as indicators that aid in the process of validating or disconfirming a provisional diagnosis of Narcissistic Disorder.

THE SCHIZOID DISORDER OF THE SELF

As with the Borderline and Narcissistic Disorders of the Self, the DSM-IV's descriptive criteria can be used to flag the Schizoid Disorder, but if rigidly adhered to, many patients with the disorder would not be diagnosed appropriately. Whereas the diagnostic criteria for Schizoid Disorder are most congruent with the symptomatology of lower-level patients, the diagnostic criteria of Avoidant Personality Disorder are most in line with the symptom picture of the upper-level Schizoid. Moving away from the DSM to the work of Harry Guntrip (1969), we find three defining behavioral clusters that mark the Schizoid personality:

1.   The *pure Schizoid cluster*, consisting of withdrawal, introversion, and lack of affect.
2.   The *Narcissistic cluster*, consisting of narcissism, superiority, and self-reliance.
3.   The *Borderline cluster*, consisting of depersonalization, regression, and loneliness.

Ralph Klein (1995) of the Masterson Institute has elaborated on the work of Guntrip in a way that has provided invaluable insights into the structure, functioning, and subjective experience of those individuals suffering a Schizoid Disorder of the Self. Klein informs us that the presence of the Schizoid cluster is a necessary (but not sufficient) condition for establishing a diagnosis of Schizoid Disorder, and that this cluster may be overt, or, as in the case of the secret Schizoid, it may be hidden, but subjectively experienced.

Other factors highlighted by Klein's work include the Schizoid individual's need to stand apart by placing himself or herself either above or below others, so that the narcissism of the Schizoid patient does not carry the same meaning as the narcissism of the Narcissistic Disorder, but rather represents a need to keep a safe distance from others by maintaining self-reliance.

In reviewing the developmental factors that play a part in the creation of Borderline and Narcissistic Disorders, Klein's work makes it clear that individuals who manifest these disorders believe that there exists a path to communication with others. For the Schizoid individual, however, the experience is that attempts at communication and connection, as well as having a self and a will of one's own will be met with appropriation, co-optation, sadistic punishment, or profound indifference. Rather than submitting to these operations, the person with a Schizoid Disorder will choose to remain apart. Subjectively, Schizoid individuals report that the only role open to them in the family was one of being a useful tool to serve the needs of the parent. Like a genie in a bottle, they were called on to be of use and then returned to oblivion. For this reason, Schizoid individuals will continually report that connection with others can only lead to an experience of being a puppet, a servant, or a slave.

The intrapsychic structure of the Schizoid Disorder of the Self (see diagram, pp. 27, 47) has been portrayed by Klein as comprising two split defensive object relations units, with the master–slave unit of attachment, the libidinal unit, consisting of a part self-representation of being a puppet or a slave, whereas the part object-representation is that of being an appropriating and co-opting master. The corresponding components of the sadistic object/self-in-exile aggressive unit, or, as Klein defines it, the unit of nonattachment, consist of a part object-representation who is sadistic, depriving, and dangerous and a part self-representation of being in exile.

Whereas those suffering a Borderline Disorder wish to be taken care of and those suffering a Narcissistic Disorder seek idealizing or mirroring supplies, the Schizoid individual's primary focus will be on the attainment of safety — which implies effecting a compromise position somewhere between the Scylla of connection and its corresponding risks of sadism and appropriation, and the Charybdis of utter isolation. For the Schizoid individual, the safest form of relationship is often found in fantasy, which protects him or her from the dangers inherent in real-life relationships while, at the same time, providing a buffer against the experience of utter aloneness.

SPLIT OBJECT RELATIONS UNIT OF THE SCHIZOID DISORDER OF THE SELF

Master Slave Part-Unit

Part Object-Representation:

a maternal part-object that is manipulative, coercive, is the master and wants to use, not relate to

AFFECT

In jail, but connected, existence acknowledged, relief in not being alienated

Part Self Representation:

a part self-representation of a dependent, a slave who provided a function for the object and is a victim

SPLITTING DEFENSE

Sadistic Object — Self-in-Exile Part-Unit

Part Object-Representation:

a maternal part-object that is sadistic, dangerous, devaluing depriving, abandoning

AFFECT
Abandonment Depression

Depression, rage, loneliness, fear of cosmic aloneness, depair

Part Self Representation:

a part self-representation of being alienated, in exile, isolated but self-contained to self-reliant

Developmental Arrest of the Ego:
Ego Defects — poor reality perception; frustration tolerance; impulse control; ego boundaries.
Primitive Ego Defense Mechanism — splitting; acting out; clinging, avoidance, denial; projection; projective identification, use of fantasy to substitute for real relationships and self-reliance.
Split Ego — reality ego plus pathological (or pleasure) ego.

For most Schizoid individuals, the unit of nonattachment is the predominant unit; however, very often, those individuals who seek treatment demonstrate issues more consistent with the libidinal unit of attachment, the master–slave unit.

In dealing with the Borderline patient, confrontation best shores up a faltering ego, whereas the Narcissistic patient will experience Mirroring Interpretations of Narcissistic Vulnerability as empathically attuned. For the Schizoid patient, effective treatment consists of interpretation of his or her Schizoid dilemma, wherein coming too close to objects results in the risk of appropriation or sadism, while moving too far from objects leads to the anguished anxiety of complete disconnection and isolation from others.

THE PSYCHOPATHIC PERSONALITY DISORDER

The psychopathic personality is notoriously unresponsive to psychodynamic treatment of any kind. However, the patient with a Psychopathic Disorder often presents himself or herself in the guise of a personality disorder, so that it is important that the therapist be able to make this differential diagnosis in order not to be caught up in an endless treatment process.

From an intrapsychic object relations perspective, in the psychopathic patient, there is no affective connection between the self and the object, which is the basis for all psychodynamic psychotherapy.

FORMULATING A DIFFERENTIAL DIAGNOSIS

As can be seen, information pertinent to the process of making a differential diagnosis is drawn from many domains. In this section, I will discuss the elements utilized in the service of building a coherent and integrated diagnostic picture. These include: (1) symptom picture; (2) family history; (3) developmental history; (4) presenting problem; (5) past and present object relations; (6) ego functioning and ego defenses; (7) self-identity; (8) transference acting out and countertransference.

1. The Symptom Picture: Axis I? Axis II? One from Axis I, One from Axis II?

The first determination a clinician must make surrounds the question of whether or not a patient's symptomatology is most consistent with a psychiatric illness, as described in Axis I of the DSM-IV; a Disorder of the Self, as described in Axis II of the DSM-IV; or a combination of the two. It is, for example, quite possible for a Borderline patient to have a concomitant Bipolar Disorder. A characteristic of symptoms related to Disorders of the Self is their reactivity to situations that reflect specific developmental issues. So, when faced with a depressed patient, a clinician must ponder whether the history of this depression is consonant with the more dynamic features of an abandonment depression that emerges each time there is a separation stress and vanishes as soon as there is reconnection with an object, a pattern consistent with the Borderline patient. Or has the loss of a prestigious position or award preceded the patient's crisis, as might be the case with a Narcissistic patient? Or does the history of the patient's depression seem less congruent with the patient's intrapsychic issues and psychodynamics and more consistent with an Axis I diagnosis of Major Depression that has appeared periodically in the patient's life, responded to medication, and followed a family history where, for example, the mother's sister was hospitalized for depression and the grandfather committed suicide?

2. Family History

"My father was an orphan," a patient told me, "so he really didn't know how to deal with people, especially his own children." Further investigation of the familial situation led to the knowledge that the patient's mother's own father was a remote man to whom she could never get close. In the patient's family, the mother spent her time controlling and micromanaging both the patient's father and the patient. With the father out of the picture and the mother oppressive, the patient indicated: "I stayed away from them both, and just tried to fend for myself, but I always wished my dad could be there more." Presumptive diagnosis: Schizoid Disorder of the Self.

A family history not only allows the clinician to become aware of medical and psychiatric information that helps in formulating a diagnosis, it also allows insight into some of the dynamics that have been transmitted down through the generations. "My mother was always running to take care of her mother," said one patient, "and I always felt sorry for her, and felt that I had to take care of her." Presumptive diagnosis: Borderline Disorder of the Self.

3. Developmental History

A detailed developmental history will also provide the clinician with significant diagnostic information. Did the patient or the patient's family suffer any losses, illnesses, or other traumas that might have put additional psychological burdens on the patient and his or her support system? If so, what developmental period was affected? How was it handled? Was the family stable? Were developmental milestones normal? Does school performance show underachieving or striving for perfection? Does the history of social interaction show a sense of alienation and a paucity of friends? Class clown behavior? Compliance with peers? What were the parents' roles in development? One patient, for example, indicated: "Whenever I didn't want to go to school, my mother would let me stay home, and we would lie in bed all day and eat and watch soap operas on TV." It was not a far leap to arrive at a presumptive diagnosis of Borderline Disorder of the Self, prompted by maternal reward for regression. Another patient stated: "My mother was always comparing me with other kids in school who were better. 'Look how well-behaved Jane is,' she'd say, or 'Matthew got such good grades in math last year.' I always felt put down by her, and it made it hard for me to feel good about myself, unless I was the best at everything." Hearing this patient's descriptions focused my attention on the ways in which his developmental circumstances were consistent with the diagnosis of Narcissistic Disorder of the Self. Similarly, a man later diagnosed with a Schizoid Disorder of the Self said of his father: "He left me with her and ran away, so that she would torture me instead of him. I longed for him to come back. I had no place to go, so I went inside."

4. Presenting Problem

All patients come into treatment with an issue to resolve. The stated issue, as well as the manner in which it is stated, and the data that are omitted are all significant in formulating a diagnosis. A 22-year-old woman was first seen in the waiting room sitting with her mother, who, I was startled to see, had her head on my patient's shoulder. "There's certainly something going on in this mother–daughter relationship," I thought to myself. Once in the consulting room, the patient proceeded to tell me how "supportive" her mother was, see how she came with her! She spoke of how well they got on, and what a "good" mother she was and had been. In taking a further history, the patient informed me she had run away from home when she was 16. When I questioned her as to why, she responded, with no emotion: "Oh, my mother used to beat me." In a very short time, I was able to see the patient's splitting in operation, and to surmise that she and her mother were engaged in relational patterns quite consistent with a diagnosis of Borderline Disorder of the Self.

In another instance, a young male patient came into my office and asked immediately if he could move his chair further away from where I was sitting. His stated issue was that he was having trouble motivating himself to write, even though he had come to New York to be a writer. However, in the course of our discussion, he also informed me that he had virtually no relationships, experienced little emotion, and rarely dreamed, and when he did, he never dreamed of other people. This initial interview was enough to alert me to the possibility of a diagnosis of Schizoid Disorder of the Self.

Often the patient's manner of presenting himself or herself is as much, or more of, a diagnostic indicator than the content being presented. Some patients will invariably open a session by asking, "How are you?" — immediately indicating the presence of a false-self operation bent on taking care of and turning to the object. Other patients may smile all the time or strive to be entertaining, while others are consistently critical, aggrieved, or condescending. Or a patient may be silent, or cryptic, or obviously anxious, treating the therapist as a harsh taskmaster or enemy. These (and all the many other) characteristic ways of behaving are defined as "characteristic" because they are indeed representative of each individual's unique character.

5. Past and Present Object Relations

A patient's adult object-relationships are telling. Has there always been clinging, as in the Borderline patient who fell in love in two weeks, and was devastated over the breakup for six months, until one day she had a new date, and was in love all over again? Or is there a significant history of idealization and/or devaluation as one might find in a Narcissistic patient? Or a paucity of relationships that might signify a Schizoid Disorder? What were early relationships like? Was the mother warm and clinging? Cold and demanding? Neglectful? Absent? Was the father there? Did he offer encouragement? Did he leave the raising to his wife? Was he perfectionistic? Abusive? Were there others in the family who provided nurturance? Were there teachers and mentors? As these data are gathered, patterns emerge that reflect the way in which the patient's early object-relationships resulted in his or her intrapsychic structure, and how, in its turn, this intrapsychic structure emerges in adult interpersonal relationships.

6. Ego Functioning and Ego Defenses

A patient's ego functioning and ego defenses serve as a guide to both the nature and the severity of his or her disorder. The patient's history of adaptive functioning offers significant diagnostic information. Thus, for Borderline patients, one might see difficulties surrounding significant points of separation or activation. Was there a dropout in the last year of high school? Difficulty with leaving home and going to college? Or did performance difficulties start even earlier? Has there been persistent self-sabotage regarding advancement at work? Or do the patient's work and school history demonstrate a continuous focus on perfect performance and severe self-criticism when it is not attained, as might be seen in a Narcissistic patient? Or has there been an absence of interest in social relationships in favor of a preoccupation with ideas and abstractions, or artistic pursuits as is often the case with Schizoid patients? Does the patient demonstrate poor judgment, and if so, in what areas? Can the patient manage his or her affect or is there a history of impulsivity? Or a need to rely heavily on external sources of support? Or a need for self-soothing through substances or other addictive behaviors? Is reality testing clouded by grandiosity or by clinging or fantasy? Do defenses include higher-level more adaptive mechanisms, such as repression, and even humor, or do you primarily see lower-level defenses, such as projection, projective identification, and denial? In session, a patient with healthier defenses and a more intact ego will be experienced as more of a whole person, able to manage life and relationships, and to be more in touch with the therapist.

7. Self-Identity

A Disorder of the Self is what its name implies. Borderline, Narcissistic, and Schizoid individuals have difficulty integrating, managing, experiencing, and expressing their real self potentials and needs. Instead, a false self will be constructed that accords with the demands of the objects as they are experienced by the child during his or her development. As we have seen, for the Exhibitionistic Narcissistic Disorder, the focus will be on maintaining an inflated sense of self and obtaining narcissistic supplies from others. In other Self Disorders, the Closet Narcissistic Disorder, the Borderline Disorder, and the Schizoid Disorder, the focus remains on the needs of the object, and far less attention is paid to the self. Said one Borderline patient, a young woman: "I don't know who I am. When I am with Her" (the tone she uses when she speaks of her mother seems to put her in caps, like God) "I feel like an ugly kid. When I'm with my dad, I feel like his girlfriend. And I turn all my teachers into mothers, so I can be a good girl." A Schizoid patient told me: "I could do something creative, I know I have the potential, but doing it would mean I have a right to exist, and I don't think I can make that statement." A Closet Narcissistic woman, married to an Exhibitionistic Narcissistic man for over 30 years, and recently divorced, told me: "I only lived through him, everything was his way. I forgot to even think about what I might want." For these patients, attachment to objects meant relinquishing healthy self-assertion and self-expression, and the joy that comes with a clear and cohesive sense of being a whole, integrated, unique, purposeful, loving, and lovable individual.

8. Transference Acting Out and Countertransference

In the course of treatment, a patient's issues will become manifest, not only in the material he or she relates regarding interaction in the world outside the consulting room, but also in the way the patient is with you; that is, in the patient's transference acting out. One patient, an Exhibitionistic Narcissistic Disorder, asked me after three or four sessions: "Now that we know each other better, what should I call you?" When I replied, "Dr. Pearson," he shot back: "Then you can call me King." A Borderline woman came into treatment in conflict about her boyfriend, and then said, "I thought last session that you wanted me to break up with him. I'm still looking for you to tell me what to do." A Schizoid woman became angry at my "intrusion" when I commented that she seemed to be working far too hard, and said, "You're pushing me. Don't tell me what to do."

As much as the patient's feelings and behaviors toward the therapist provide information, so too do the therapist's feelings and behaviors toward the patient, because the kind of reaction we have to a patient more often than not is a major diagnostic indicator. In one case, for example, a woman patient presented with all the hallmarks of a Closet Narcissistic Disorder, but I kept feeling I could not reach her. I was frustrated, baffled, and sad, as I continued to experience a wall between us. Finally, I tried some interpretations more consonant with a Schizoid diagnosis, and the patient woke up and the treatment took off. In another instance, a man in his 50s was complaining reasonably about a woman he had been seeing, and I kept hearing his balanced tone, but having images in my mind of his beating her up. I finally asked him if he wasn't angry with her, after which several months went by when we addressed nothing but his rage toward women. A woman talked in a flat voice about how, in childhood, she had lived with her mother, who never talked to her, and I had an image in my head of Wyeth's painting "Christina's World" — an image that let me tune in to her desolation.

The issues raised by the transference–countertransference choreography engaged in by both patient and therapist in the course of a treatment are perhaps the most complex, substantive, and fascinating elements of analytic work, with roots, it is now being demonstrated, that go deep into our neurobiologic, as well as our psychological, selves. These arenas, compelling and significant as they may be, cannot be done justice here. With regard, however, to differential diagnosis, suffice it to say that some part of that process will be accomplished through active cognition, pulling together all the bits and pieces of information one has about the patient and about the theory. But some piece of who the patient is, and what he or she needs, will always be communicated in ways that lie beyond the pale of conscious recognition, unfolding as explicated knowledge for both participants only through consistent therapeutic elucidation of the patient–therapist dynamic that lies at the heart of the work.

5

THE BORDERLINE PERSONALITY DISORDER

Arlene Hahn, C.S.W.

Lynn, age 24, was referred to an outpatient psychiatric clinic for psychotherapy following a brief hospitalization for an overdose of an over-the-counter medication. She compensated almost immediately after her admission, and was no longer suicidal. She had had one prior admission following a suicidal gesture and has a history of polysubstance abuse and self-mutilation. All destructive acts have been impulsive; she is prone to temper outbursts and complains of feeling empty inside. Both hospitalizations followed breakups with boyfriends. She has episodic dysphoria, which lasts a few days. She has difficulty keeping a job because of absenteeism and she exploded at customers when working as a cashier.

Lynn has been diagnosed with Borderline Personality Disorder, meeting the DSM-IV criteria.

Rachel is a 28-year-old woman who works as a production assistant for a film company. She moved back to New York City to live with her parents following the failure of her video rental store in Connecticut, which she had owned for over a year. She blames the failure on the location and her poor choice of partner. Prior to her return, she discovered that her former boyfriend had become engaged. She was devastated by the news and felt depressed, helpless, and hopeless. Within a month of her return to New York, she had met a man at a job interview with whom she immediately became involved, and felt much better. This relationship has ended, leaving her depressed and concerned that she will fail at her new job, where she is having difficulty with her boss. Rachel came to therapy stating, "I'm feeling depressed and want to break patterns that leave me starting over again."

Rachel has been diagnosed with Borderline Personality Disorder, but does not meet DSM-IV criteria.

DSM-IV Diagnosis Criteria for Borderline Personality Disorder

A pervasive pattern of instability of interpersonal relationships, self-image, and affects, and marked impulsivity beginning in early adulthood and present in a variety of contexts, as indicated by five (or more) of the following.

1. Frantic efforts to avoid real or imagined abandonment
2. A pattern of unstable and intense interpersonal relationships characterized by alternating between extremes of idealization and devaluation
3. Identity disturbance: markedly and persistently unstable self-image or sense of self
4. Impulsivity in at least two areas that are potentially self-damaging
5. Recurrent suicidal behaviors, gestures or threats, or self-mutilating behavior
6. Affective instability due to a marked reactivity of mood (e.g., intense episodic dysphoria, irritability, or anxiety usually lasting a few hours and only rarely more than a few days)
7. Chronic feelings of emptiness
8. Inappropriate, intense anger or difficulty controlling anger (e.g., frequent displays of temper, constant anger, recurrent physical fights)
9. Transient, stress-related paranoid ideation or severe dissociative symptoms

How can these two patients with such different presentations and levels of functioning have the same diagnosis?

Masterson cites a study by Weston and Arkowitz-Weston, who report that 60% of patients who come to treatment with personality disorder pathology were not diagnosable on DSM-IV Axis II (Masterson, 2000, p. 63).

The DSM-IV diagnostic category for the Borderline Personality Disorder is a descriptive diagnosis with criteria that focus on obvious symptoms and behavior. It does not differentiate between levels of functioning, emphasizing symptoms of lower-level Borderline patients. Higher-level patients are likely to be diagnosed as Neurotic. The DSM-IV does not address intrapsychic structure.

THE MASTERSON APPROACH TO DIAGNOSIS
OF THE BORDERLINE PERSONALITY DISORDER

The developmental and psychodynamic approach formulated by Masterson facilitates diagnosis and clinical application (Masterson, 2000, pp. 55–56). The components of diagnosis from a developmental self and object relations approach include:

1. DSM-IV symptoms
2. Separation–individuation stress, loss of parent, separation/divorce, going away to

college, a sibling leaving home, and other individuation stresses that pose challenges about capacity, self-reliance, and separation

3. The intrapsychic structure as outlined in the history of relationships with others and with the therapist
4. The developmental arrested ego seen in the primitive defense mechanisms and defects in ego functioning
5. The Disorder of the Self Triad, confirmed by confrontation.

RACHEL

(To highlight the Masterson Approach to theory, diagnosis, and treatment, I will refer to the case of Rachel throughout this chapter.)

Rachel has a long history of problems at work and school. She never realized her potential, finding ways to manipulate the system in order to get by. When she was 26, at the recommendation of her former therapist, she was tested and diagnosed with mild learning disabilities, which explained her difficulties with reading. The patient found this diagnosis to be a relief and enormously helpful in understanding her academic struggles, but she was angry that it had not been discovered earlier, given its negative impact on her self-esteem.

Rachel's mother was diagnosed with breast cancer and had a bilateral mastectomy when Rachel was 6 years old. The family never discussed it and Rachel, concerned and frightened, was left to deal with it on her own. She describes her mother as feisty, intelligent, strong, sensitive, and capable, but as never living up to her potential. She was her mother's confidant, and believes that she was the only one who understood her. She thinks her mother was far too revealing about the details of her dissatisfaction with Rachel's father. She believes that they were enmeshed and that her mother feared losing her, utilizing money as a threat and means of control.

Rachel's father is seen as an insecure, compassionate, stubborn, and complicated man with limited insight. He is a talented musician who had difficulty promoting himself. He relied on his wife to manage the business aspects of his career, and Rachel thinks he also had learning disabilities. He demonstrated little interest in the patient and her activities, favoring her older sister, with whom he shared musical interests.

Rachel's sister is married and is an advertising account executive. She is described as jealous, and tormented the patient as a child by taunting and criticizing her and taking her possessions. The patient wanted her acceptance and approval, but would feel pulled in and then pushed away.

The patient was a good student until the third grade, when she began to have difficulties with reading and completing assignments. By middle school, the teachers viewed her as lazy; however, when she applied herself, she was able to earn good grades. She had many friends and was involved in after-school activities, including ballet, gymnastics, and art, but lost interest when she was unable to achieve instant mastery.

In high school, Rachel resorted to plagiarism, copying an essay from *Cliff's Notes* in order to keep up. She wanted to become an actor, began auditioning at age 14, and appeared in a television commercial. Her mother discouraged her acting and withheld the money she needed to take professional acting classes. The patient thinks her mother was jealous of her looks and was ashamed of her own body following the mastectomy. Rachel's interest in acting declined when she became involved with a boy at school. She had several boyfriends in high school and became sexually active at age 16.

Rachel attended college in New England, where she received a bachelor's degree in media production. She applied herself the first year and did well until she began smoking marijuana. Her grades dropped and, frightened of failing, she again resorted to plagiarism, borrowing notes, and purchasing papers. She felt like an "imposter," but could not risk failing. She had several brief relationships during college.

Following college, Rachel worked briefly for an independent film company and held several retail jobs, including a manager's position at a video rental store. She traveled to the West Coast and moved in with a college boyfriend. When they broke up, she called her parents to ask for money so that she could return home. She lived in their country house in Connecticut and worked as an aide in a children's service agency.

Rachel met Sam at a bar when she was 24. She thought she was in love, and within two months, they were living together, whereupon their relationship changed. Sam supported her while she took care of the house and Sam's needs. Although she liked feeling needed, Sam was extremely critical and emotionally unavailable. In addition, Sam did not conceal the fact that he was still seeing other women.

Rachel entered therapy for the first time when she was living with Sam and had become depressed and anxious that he would leave her. In therapy, recognizing how dysfunctional the relationship was, she left him and moved back to her parents' house in Connecticut. Feeling good about her retail skills, she opened a video rental store in a nearby town with a woman friend from college and moved out of her parents' home. Unable to succeed in her retail business, she returned to New York to live with her parents. It was at this time that she received the news that Sam, her former boyfriend, was getting married.

Upon returning to New York, she met Matt at a job interview and became involved in an "emotional roller-coaster." It lasted three months, and the patient was devastated and disbelieving when he left. The patient believes she selects men who cannot commit and she provides care and attention as a way of holding on: "I find out what people want and give it to them." Since her return to New York, she has been working as a production assistant in the film industry. Her boss yells at her and belittles her publicly. She earns a low salary, but is interested in learning to produce documentary films.

I. Problems at Work and with Relationships

Adults with a diagnosis of Borderline Personality Disorder usually enter psychotherapy in their 20s to 30s because of a separation stress, loss, panic, depression, or problems with intimacy. It is the time in life when their difficulties at work and with relationships become apparent. Although the chaotic lives of lower-level Borderline patients are obvious, higher-level Borderline individuals function better and may appear successful to the outside world. However, one only has to scratch the surface for problems with self-activation and intimacy to come to the forefront.

Children with Borderline Disorders are rarely seen, since their symptoms are masked by childhood dependency on the family. Adolescents may be seen because of behavior problems or anorexia. Midlife may also precipitate a crisis for those who begin to feel that they are dissatisfied with their lives.

All individuals with a Borderline Personality Disorder have problems with self-activation, have forfeited their real selves, and live primarily in defense. Self-activation triggers affects of the abandonment depression. The real self has not developed, and capacities of the self are lacking or impaired. The false self defends against the abandonment depression and is in operation most of the time.

In the work arena, individuals who appear to be successful may not actually be achieving their potential. They may be dissatisfied with their jobs or employed below their skill levels. Career choices may have resulted from family expectations ("Everyone just assumed I would be a lawyer, I never questioned it"). Real talents, capabilities, and creativity may be avoided and undeveloped.

In the relationship arena, fears of engulfment or abandonment prevent real intimacy from developing. Clinging and/or distancing defenses are utilized to defend against these feelings. Clinging, more typical in the higher-level Borderline individual, is an attempt to hold on to the significant object. These patients may seek out partners who collude with their avoidance of separation and individuation. They have a distorted view of others and tend to paint a rosy picture, ignoring red flags that indicate impending problems. They will settle for crumbs of acknowledgment and support.

The Borderline patient feels unable to manage his or her own life in a mature manner. He or she feels dependent and looks to others for caretaking and gratification of needs. This patient has deficits in attachment, is not autonomous, and has not achieved the level of separation and individuation necessary to function as a mature adult. He or she feels immature and younger than his or her chronological years. Self-activation provokes intense and painful affects of depression and anxiety, and therefore is avoided.

The real self of the Borderline individual is impaired and thwarted, more in some individuals than others. His or her emotional life is riddled with anger, and he or she is frustrated by the inability to self-activate and express himself or herself. Impairments may exist in spontaneity and aliveness of affect, self-entitlement, self-activation, assertion and support, acknowledgment of self-activation and maintenance of self-esteem; continuity of self, commitment, creativity, intimacy, and autonomy (Masterson, 2000, p. 54).

II. DEVELOPMENTAL ARREST

Masterson pinpoints the origin of the Borderline Personality Disorder as a developmental arrest in the rapprochement subphase of Mahler's model for the separation–individuation phases of preoedipal development. The rapprochement subphase occurs approximately between 15 and 22 months of age, when the toddler has achieved a sense of individuality and separateness from the mother and seeks her out to share a growing pleasurable sense of difference. The rapprochement crisis, commonly known as the "terrible two's," revolves around the toddler's ambivalence about doing for himself or herself or letting the mother do it. As omnipotence and grandiosity are diminishing, emotions become differentiated, with increased awareness of feelings, particularly of sadness and longing. The developmental arrest in the rapprochement subphase is a result of failures in nature, nurture, and fate. Nurturing failure, stemming from defects in maternal libidinal availability, implies the mother's difficulty in providing emotional supplies and support for individuation. For example, a Borderline mother may cling to the child and reward regressive behavior as a way of defending against her own anxiety and abandonment issues, which have not been addressed. The Borderline mother is available for regression and unavailable for individuation. Conversely, a Borderline mother may be uncomfortable with the child's dependency and promote premature separation.

The father of a Borderline child is typically uninvolved with the mother–child relationship and does not rescue the child from these interactions. He is usually absorbed in work or interests that keep him away from home and are not opposed by the mother.

Nurturing failure may occur, not only as a consequence of the mother's separation issues, but also because of physical illness or absenteeism. Nature and fate, such as the child's illness or external situations beyond control, may also have an impact on development, regardless of parental effectiveness.

These interactions are internalized and become incorporated into the child's intrapsychic structure, producing the object relations unit of the Borderline individual. One must keep in mind that it is the individual's perception of the mother's withdrawal that is introjected. Although some theorists tend to minimize the role of the mother, Masterson believes that the mother's difficulty in supporting the toddler's emerging self during the rapprochement phase is a key element in the developmental arrest. He views the arrest as a pathological arrest of the self, with associated arrest of the ego and the object relations.

III. THE INTRAPSYCHIC STRUCTURE

The intrapsychic structure of individuals with a Borderline Disorder is the most enduring and fixed aspect of their disorder. In the Borderline individual, the intrapsychic structure can be viewed as a quadrant divided into two units, each with two parts (see diagram, p. 62).

The split object relations unit includes a good self and object-representation, referred to as the rewarding object relations part-unit, or the RORU, and a bad self- and object-representation, referred to as the withdrawing object relations part-unit, or the WORU. Each part-unit is composed of a self-representation and an object-representation.

In the rewarding part-unit, the maternal part object is approving and rewarding of regressive behavior. The part self-representation is of a good, passive, compliant child, who is linked by the affects of feeling good, and being taken care of, loved, fed, and gratified by the wish for reunion.

In the withdrawing part-unit, the maternal part object withdraws, attacks, and is angry and critical of efforts at separation and individuation. The part self-representation is one of feeling bad, inadequate, ugly, and defective. The affect linking the self- and object-representations is the abandonment depression. The formation of the split object relations unit occurs during interactions between the child and the mother. The child's perceptions of self and mother, combined with the affect that links these images, are internalized. These become intrapsychic images of self and significant other, as well as the feelings associated with these images.

The part-units can alternate according to the individual's affective state, with the rewarding unit usually the more dominant of the two. These conflicting images remain conscious, but do not influence each other. From childhood, the Borderline individual relates to people as parts, positive and negative, rather than as whole, and is unable to establish a single unified reality concept of self and other.

The split object relations unit is also accompanied by a developmental arrest of the ego, resulting in poor reality perception, low frustration tolerance, poor impulse control, and inadequate ego boundaries. Primitive ego defense mechanisms are present, including splitting, acting out, clinging, avoidance, denial, projection, and projective identification.

The Borderline patient's split ego combines a reality ego that deals with the demands of reality and a pathological or pleasure ego that seeks gratification through fantasy and denial. The Borderline individual is unable to fuse these images into one

SPLIT OBJECT RELATIONS UNIT OF THE BORDERLINE

Rewarding or Libidinal Part-Unit (RORU)

Part Object-Representation:

 a maternal part-object that offers approval of regressive and clinging behavior

AFFECT

feeling good   being fed
being taken care of   gratifying the wish for
being loved   reunion

Part Self Representation:

 a part self-representation of being the good, passive child — unique and special/grandiose

(center vertical label: SPLITTING DEFENSE)

Withdrawing or Aggressive Part-Unit (WORU)

Part Object-Representation:

 a maternal part-object that withdraws, is angry and critical of efforts toward separation–individuation

AFFECT
Abandonment Depression

homicidal rage   hopelessness and helplessness
suicidal depression   emptiness and void
panic   guilt

Part Self Representation:

 a part self-representation of being inadequate, bad, ugly, an insect, etc.

Developmental Arrest of the Ego:
Ego Defects — poor reality perception; frustration tolerance; impulse control; ego boundaries.
Primitive Ego Defense Mechanism — splitting; acting out; clinging, avoidance, denial; projection; projective identification.
Split Ego — reality ego plus pathological (or pleasure) ego.

and perceives the self and the mother as whole constant individuals. For those individuals who progress further along the developmental continuum, the split fantasy does not last. As the child separates from the mother, split objects fuse into whole objects and repression replaces splitting. The mother who yells is the same mother who hugs. The child who breaks a dish is the same child who learns to drink from a cup.

IV. Higher- vs. Lower-Level Borderline Personality Disorders

1. Lower-Level Borderline Adult

The lower-level Borderline individual has an earlier developmental arrest and his or her behavior is akin to the DSM-IV criteria. The patient exhibits more self-destructive behavior; has defenses that are more primitive, and his or her functioning is less adaptive.

> As a rule, the earlier the onset of the developmental arrest, the more severe will be the manifestations of the Borderline Personality Disorder. ... the earlier the onset of the arrest, the less intrapsychic structure there is in place, and, as the term *arrest* implies, no further development takes place. ... the child, early in rapprochement, has only recently emerged from the more or less absolute dependence on the "self-regulating" functions of the "other" ... projection, projective identification, splitting (primitive immature defenses), and withdrawal and distancing (defenses against the dread of absolute dependence and engulfment) are common. The WORU is the major projection of the lower-level patient (Klein, 1989, p. 149).

2. Higher-Level Borderline Adult

The higher-level Borderline individual has a later developmental arrest and a more developed intrapsychic structure. Splitting is still a major defense, but he or she is further along the developmental continuum. Defenses ward off fears of abandonment rather than fears of engulfment. The projection of the RORU is dominant and the patient utilizes denial, clinging, and avoidance defenses.

V. Abandonment Depression

The abandonment depression of the Borderline individual is composed of affects of homicidal rage, suicidal depression, panic, hopelessness and helplessness, emptiness and void, and guilt. It is always an underlying threat and is kept at bay by clinging and foregoing self-activation in exchange for superficially feeling good. As a result, the Borderline individual develops a deflated false self, which is based on both a fantasy that people provide support for clinging and avoidance of self-activation, and a bad self-image of weakness and insecurity. He or she may act out to obtain instant gratification, feel good, and avoid the affects of the abandonment depression through excessive work, substance abuse, and sex and/or instant relationships.

VI. Disorders of the Self Triad

Attempts to self-activate precipitate the abandonment depression and cause the Borderline individual to live primarily in defense.

The patient's efforts at self-activation lead to separation anxiety and abandonment depression, which lead to defense. In other words, efforts at self-activation, including participation in therapy, precipitate the withdrawing unit with its abandonment depression. To defend against this unit, the patient has two options. A pathological ego through the alliance with the rewarding unit can activate that unit. The patient gives up self-activation under the sway of the rewarding unit and is able to deny that he or she is behaving regressively and maladaptively. If the alliance is with the withdrawing unit, the patient activates the withdrawing unit and massively projects and acts it out, either with a distancing form of transference acting out or as external acting out. Seemingly, the patient has a Hobson's choice, either to feel bad and abandoned, or to defend against that feeling at the cost of adaptation to reality (Masterson, 2000, p. 55).

VII. SPLITTING

Splitting is a primary defense against the abandonment depression. The splitting defense separates the contradictory images of good and bad mother and good and bad child, and the associated feeling states of being loved and rejected. Themes of rewarding for clinging and withdrawal for separation are embedded in the intrapsychic structure.

VIII. DIFFERENTIAL DIAGNOSIS

As the therapist listens to the history, assesses ego functioning and defenses, and observes the patient, he or she distinguishes among the different personality disorders in order to make an initial diagnosis. The diagnosis will determine the approach to utilize, followed by a trial of the approach to confirm the diagnosis.

The following describes the differential diagnostic process for the case of Rachel.

Rachel is experiencing separation stress related to the sudden ending of a relationship. She has become more aware of her great difficulty in establishing healthy relationships and has identified a pattern of involvement with unavailable men. Her history reveals an inability to activate, a deflated self-image, acting out by trying to establish instant intimacy, clinging, impulsivity, and impaired ego functioning. She looks to objects to manage her anxiety, with a wish to be taken care of. Issues appear to be preoedipal and related to abandonment and problems with separation and individuation. The patient has symptoms of mild depression; Major Affective Disorder was ruled out. My initial diagnostic impression was Borderline Personality Disorder, which was quickly confirmed by the patient's response to confrontations.

Neurosis was ruled out, since issues are not oedipal and the patient does not exhibit whole object relations.

Narcissistic Disorder was ruled out because of the patient's concern with gaining control over her life, rather than looking for perfect mirroring or fusion with the object. She had not expressed concern over falling apart. In addition, I saw no evidence of grandiosity, idealization, or investment in an omnipotent other.

Schizoid Disorder was ruled out since the patient was not consumed by a need for space or a fear of reliance on others accompanied by deep cravings for relating.

Psychosis was ruled out, since reality resting was intact and there is no evidence of thought disorder or a history of psychotic symptoms.

IX PSYCHOTHERAPY

When the Borderline patient begins treatment, his or her primary motivation is to find a therapist who will help him or her to feel better, rather than get better. However, there is a wish, albeit buried and small, that is a manifestation of the patient's impaired real self's desire to grow and become a healthier, mature individual.

1. Treatment Goals

The goals for the Borderline patient in shorter-term treatment, exemplified by the case of Rachel, include containment of acting out with verbalization of affects, improved ego functioning and adaptation, and an increase in self-activation.

2. Transference Acting Out

When the Borderline patient begins psychotherapy, he or she does not have the capacity to see the therapist as a whole separate individual, which restricts the capacity to form the transference required for a therapeutic alliance.

The Borderline transference is not simply transference, but transference acting out, which consists of the alternate activation and projection on the therapist of each of the split object relations part-units. Both, however, represent forms of transference acting out, an instant replay, in which the therapist is treated not as a real object upon whom infantile feelings are displaced, but as if he or she actually were the infantile object. It differs from a transference psychosis in that the patient has the capacity to distinguish between the projection and the reality of the therapist when it is brought to his or her attention (Masterson, 1981, p. 149).

As a result, a goal of therapy is to convert transference acting out into therapeutic alliance and transference. When patients enter treatment, they lead with the projections of either the WORU or the RORU.

Clinical example: During the first month of treatment, as Rachel pursued men in a desperate manner, it became clear that she jumped into relationships, ignored red flags, and sought instant intimacy, assuming that any new involvement was a serious relationship. I hypothesized that she acted out by incorporating her clinging defense to avoid feeling her abandonment depression. The patient related to me in a similar manner when she informed me in the first session that I was the therapist for her. The patient entered treatment projecting the RORU.

3. Confrontation

Confrontation of the self-destructive maladaptive defenses is the therapeutic approach with the Borderline patient to establish a therapeutic alliance. It is a therapeutic intervention that addresses the primitive defenses of splitting, avoidance, and denial by empathically bringing the patient face to face with the maladaptive functioning of his or her defenses. It is generally directed at the self-destructive aspects of the patient's life. Confrontation facilitates the patient's conscious awareness of the behaviors and affects that have been split off and denied. It causes the behavior to become ego-dystonic, as it disrupts the patient's defensive operation and creates conflict where there was not any previously. Confrontation may take different forms, depending on the style and personality of the therapist and the patient's psychological and therapeutic needs. At times, it may even take the form of silence with a patient who is always looking to the therapist to take over. No matter which form is utilized, it must be in the therapeutic interests of the patient. Therapeutic neutrality, frame, and stance are fundamental to the treatment approach and are necessary for confrontation to be effective.

> Confrontation must be done intuitively and empathically and must "fit" the clinical material the patient presents. It requires that the therapist confront from a neutral, objective, emotional stance because it is clinically indicated, not out of anger or from his or her own personal needs, that is, to be aggressive and assertive, to direct, control, or admonish the patient (Masterson, 1981, p. 136).

The tactics the therapist employs in confrontation generally fall into four categories, which overlap clinically and can seldom be sharply differentiated.

1. Limit setting;
2. Reality testing;

3. Clarifying the consequences of maladaptive thoughts, feelings, or behaviors;
4. Questioning the motivation for maladaptive thoughts, feelings, or behaviors.

Whatever the form of confrontation, the task of the therapist is to ally himself or herself with the patient's impaired real self and reality ego by stripping away layer upon layer of distortion created by the patient's false, defensive self and pathological ego structure (Klein, 1989, p. 220).

Confrontation is successful when the patient integrates it by looking at the destructiveness of his or her behavior, and begins questioning, and eventually changing, that behavior. However, this occurs over time. Confrontation also activates the Disorder of the Self Triad while the patient is learning to manage the associated affects of the abandonment depression. The therapist must consistently utilize confrontation when the patient is in defense or the therapy will slow down. If the therapist forfeits the approach, therapy will come to a halt. Confrontation should only be utilized when the patient is in defense. The therapist's confrontations should match the level of intensity of the defense. The stronger the defense, the more vigorous should be the confrontations. If the patient responds by utilizing and incorporating the confrontations, the therapist has confirmation of the diagnosis of Borderline Personality Disorder.

Clinical Example of Confrontation of the RORU Defense
(Case of Rachel, Months 1–3)

Rachel was preoccupied with the loss of her last boyfriend. The relationship had been based on sex and the patient misconstrued this as intimacy, thinking that they were mutually committed and in love. She was finding it intolerable to be without a relationship and worried that she would never meet someone who truly cared for her. Within a month she had met a new man, and after one date, told me he was terrific, mature, and right for her. I decided to confront her poor judgment and wish for instant intimacy and asked, "How do you know he is the right man for you, when you just met him?" The patient responded, "He was so nice to me, but I guess I don't know him yet." The man didn't call as promised, yet the patient still pursued him. I confronted her clinging behavior and disregard of the man's unavailability: "You say you're tired of always being involved with men who can't commit, yet you ignore red flags and pursue him anyway." The patient responded, "I guess I want a relationship so badly I ignore the obvious so I don't have to be alone. I've always been the one to do all the work; that was my role in my family. I can't really imagine that someone would be there for me. My parents were always consumed with their own lives and never knew, or were interested in, what was going on with me."

Clinical Example of Confrontation of the WORU Defense
(Case of Rachel, Months 4–6)

During the next few months, Rachel talked about her wish for a relationship with a man who would be better for her, someone who would love her and was not just interested in sex. She attempted dating, which was a new experience, giving her the opportunity to determine her interest in someone. Simultaneously, she became more dissatisfied with her job, where she was poorly treated by her boss. She had no man in her life to provide a defense and began to fantasize about her old boyfriend, the man who had rejected her just before she began treatment. When she considered calling him, again I confronted her: "You've told me so many times how much Matt hurt you and, instead of dealing with your feelings about being alone, you're considering going right back into the same situation."

The patient's response was defensive: "I wouldn't get involved, I just want to see him as a friend." I continued to confront her defensive response: "Who are you trying to fool now?" The patient seemed to integrate the confrontation and responded with affect: "I know it would be a bad move, I never realized how hard it is for me to be alone. I've always been in a relationship and know I need to learn to be alone. I felt so desperate I tried to fool myself." She soon met a man from London who was on vacation and spent a week with him. She did not report this until the man had left, in order to maintain this defense. I first confronted her acting out by asking, "Why have you waited to tell me?" The patient admitted she wanted to do it without any interference. I continued to confront and asked, "How are you going to work on this problem if you keep it out of therapy?" She responded, "I don't see any harm, I had a good time and it's better than being alone." Still in defense, I confronted again: "Sounds like a quick fix." The patient became angry, saying, "There is nothing wrong with some fun." She was projecting the WORU and was unable to see the therapy or me as helpful. At the next session, the patient said she had realized during the week that this behavior wouldn't help and only gave her a temporary fix. With affect, she discussed her desperation and fears of being alone.

Consistency in Confrontation, Integration, and Self-Activation
(Case of Rachel, Months 7–9)

The focus during these months shifted to work and Rachel's anger at her abusive boss. I confronted: "How come you let him talk to you that way?" Response: "I've always tried to please people and wind up being mistreated. I do a good job and he's lucky to have me. I would never treat anyone the way he's treating me." The patient integrated the confrontation and began standing up to her boss, and was surprised when he backed down. She was pleased and began to focus on her abilities and how she was not achieving what she would like for herself.

The patient began to look for other jobs, but repeated the same pattern she had with men. She was willing to take a job because it was offered, even when inappropriate, and then made it sound like the perfect position. I confronted this pattern: "You seem to do this with men as well as with jobs. In both circumstances, you're willing to begin without exploring whether it's right for you and then sell it to yourself. In fact, you sell yourself short and risk winding up in another situation without a future, which is exactly the opposite of what you say you want for yourself." The patient responded with affect and talked about how her mother was bitter following her illness and never supported her talent and ambition, ignored her interests, and even put her down.

4. Tracking the Triad

The therapist asks himself or herself what's on center stage. He or she can determine if the patient is self-activating, is feeling the affects of the abandonment depression, or is in defense.

The triad can be tracked throughout the session, and at any point in treatment. This process is an extremely useful tool for the therapist, permitting him or her to know when to intervene. It is also a way of tracking the patient's progress.

Clinical Example (Case of Rachel, Months 9–10)

Self-activation was on center stage a great deal during this phase. Rachel's self-activation and movement toward increased separation and individuation led to affects associated with the abandonment depression; she employed pathological defense mechanisms to feel good, primarily by complying with the object, acting out, and clinging.

Rachel stood up to her boss and began to look for another job. In addition to seeking another job, she began to develop freelance work. In her free time, she sent out resumes and joined a women's business association in order to network. As I anticipated, she moved along the Disorder of the Self Triad from self-activation, to depression, to defense. She expressed anxiety and said she felt depressed. The patient was tempted to contact her former boyfriend, Matt, after a chance encounter, and tried to convince me, as well as herself, that he had changed now that he was in therapy. Aware that defense was back on center stage, I confronted her maladaptive thoughts.

5. Countertransference Acting Out

The Borderline patient enters treatment projecting the RORU or WORU of the object relations unit and attempts to engage the therapist in an instant replay of the past. Masterson refers to the therapist's responses to the patient's transference acting out as countertransference acting out.

The most common pitfall is seen when the therapist steps into the rewarding unit of the patient, since this is the most frequent projection. The therapist resonates consciously or unconsciously with the projection and acts out the object-representation of the RORU. The therapist becomes the regressive "good" object by taking over significant functions for the patient. Although the patient and the therapist may receive temporary gratification, treatment stops.

The Borderline patient who is projecting the WORU is trying to rid himself or herself of negative and painful affects. This is often a result of the therapist's not colluding with the RORU projection. The therapist who resonates with these projections may feel, and act out, the rejecting, cold, withholding, "bad" object. When this occurs, the therapist and patient may act out the rewarding unit to feel better, or one, or both, may withdraw. The patient may react to the therapist's withdrawal by leaving treatment.

The best protection against the therapist's countertransference acting out is to understand the intrapsychic structure of the patient. At times, feelings will be evoked, even in the experienced therapist, and clinical understanding and self-awareness are necessary tools for responding in a therapeutic manner.

Clinical Example (Case of Rachel, also Months 8–10)

Rachel felt more confident and wanted to form her own production company. She did not appear to be acting impulsively, but I was concerned as to whether or not this was a realistic venture and whether she had the capacity to go out on her own. I believed my concern was a consequence of the patient's projective identification of the withdrawing mother who did not support her self-activation. Recognizing this possibility, I did not resonate with the projection, deciding to remain silent and let things unfold, without interfering with the patient's self-activation.

Therapeutic Alliance (Case of Rachel, Months 11–13)

As the treatment moved along, Rachel was able to leave her job, and she started a small business venture with financial backing she solicited from an investor in the film industry. After the initial excitement of leaving her job, the patient was surprised by her depression. Unable to tolerate the waves of abandonment depression, she defended against it by resuming contact with Matt. In session, she began to confront herself by questioning her destructive behavior and acknowledging her avoidance of feelings related to being on her own. This was a turning point in treatment and appeared to be the beginning of a therapeutic alliance.

Emerging Real Self (Case of Rachel, Months 16–18)

Rachel moved rapidly on the production of her own documentary and was extremely resourceful and creative. The documentary received an excellent review. She brought copies of the documentary and the review into session, stating that she wanted me to see her success, that for the first time in her life, she felt "real," could take care of herself and no longer was an "imposter." Following the success of the first documentary, she produced two more, and then decided not to renew her contract with the investor, who received 50% of the profits. She applied for a small business loan and took a part-time job in the film industry in order to continue her own business.

In the interpersonal arena, Rachel is now dating without jumping into relationships. She is evaluating the men she meets to determine if there are any red flags.

She is addressing her separation issues, including financial reliance on her parents and the fear of being on her own.

6. Shorter-Term vs. Longer-Term Intensive Psychotherapy

Decisions about the duration and frequency of treatment are based on practical matters, such as time and money, as well as on the patient's motivation and capacity.

Shorter-term therapy is very effective for many Borderline patients. Treatment may last anywhere from six months to two years and sessions are held one to two times per week. Confrontation is the technique employed, and it yields substantial results. Gains are made in the patient's self-image and the management of his or her life. The patient achieves a healthier level of adaptation, ego functioning, and self-activation. Although the abandonment depression is not worked through, the patient learns to contain his or her acting out, to verbalize feelings, and to develop constructive outlets to manage painful affects. The patient is still at risk during periods when there are separation stresses, and may need to return to treatment at a later date.

In longer-term intensive treatment, the patient is seen a minimum of three times per week over three to five years.

> Intensive analytic psychotherapy ... has as its primary goal to remove the defenses against the abandonment depression and to reactivate the real self in order to bring on the abandonment depression in full force for the purpose of working it through in the close therapeutic relationship. The preliminary goal is to create the therapeutic alliance and transference and remove the pathological defenses that prevent the depression. ... The patient realizes in the final working-through, however, that it was not the separation stresses that caused problems over the years, but the unavailability of maternal support at his initial efforts to separate and express his real self (Masterson, 1988, p. 136).

Confrontation is the main intervention until acting out is contained. The working-through of the abandonment depression requires interpretation as memories emerge. As a result of intensive therapy, ego functions mature and healthier defenses are formed. The patient is able to lead a healthier, more productive, self-assertive, and fulfilling life. The real self is no longer subject to the threat of the abandonment depression and separation stress. As the patient's split object relations units consolidate, intrapsychic structural change results. The patient is able to perceive objects as whole, both good and bad, facilitating separation and individuation, and is on the road to achieving, or achieves, object constancy.

6

THE NARCISSISTIC PERSONALITY DISORDER

Anne R. Lieberman, L.C.S.W.

A certain amount of narcissism is a necessary component of a healthy personality. It provides us with healthy self-esteem, which then enables us to negotiate our relationships, our jobs, and our creativity in satisfying and meaningful ways. Too little can leave us feeling inadequate, unworthy, unlovable. Too much and we can turn into grandiose exhibitionists with little regard for anyone else.

Narcissism can be described as the libidinal investment in the self. Normal narcissism is necessary to regulate self-esteem and to pursue interests and ambitions. It is reality based; encompasses self-satisfaction experienced as self-esteem, confidence, and a general sense of well-being; and includes appropriate concern for others. Narcissism moves to the pathological when it becomes self-centered, self-involved, lacking in empathy.

The Masterson Approach, recognizing the underlying intrapsychic structure of the patient, enables the therapist to understand and determine the ways in which the patient perceives and relates to the world. This structure becomes pathological when it is fixed and chronic; repeats itself over and over, independent of the external environment; is based on fantasy; and defends against affect, rather than dealing with reality. It has strengths and weaknesses, which serve both adaptive and maladaptive purposes. Originally, it was not necessarily pathological; rather, it was the child's response to developmental issues. At one time, the defenses served a purpose. The problem is that they became fixed and rigid. In the Narcissistic Personality Disorder, the intrapsychic structure of the patient provides a sense of specialness and uniqueness by either identification with or idealization of the object in order to ward off underlying feelings of humiliation, shame, and fragmentation.

It is possible that some Exhibitionistic Narcissistic pathology is the most adaptive disorder in today's world. The nature and rhythm of the disorder are consistent with the pleasure principle. Those with such personality structures will appear to have more rewards in terms of success, money, fame, and so on, for example, entertainers, politicians, and sports stars. Therefore, it is also quite possible that most of these people are not in therapy offices. If they appear that successful and functional, society does not see them as disordered. They only come into therapy when fate is unkind, causing the intrapsychic structure to collapse so that it no longer works to protect them from the painful affects of the underlying abandonment depression. Often, once their sense of the world's resonating with their needs is restored, they leave treatment. They seek treatment, as do all patients with a Disorder of the Self, to *feel* better, not necessarily to *get* better.

The following presentations introduce two patients who will be followed throughout the chapter to illustrate two of the different faces of the Narcissistic Personality Disorder. Harry is a married man, the father of two sons. He works as an accountant. The president of his neighborhood association, he likes to be in charge and to decide how things are to be run. In his marriage, he is sure that he knows what works best for the family; he makes financial choices and child-rearing decisions, he likes to approve of his wife's purchases, and has difficulty tolerating differences of opinion. At work, he takes charge, often inappropriately, and he repeatedly loses jobs because he has difficulty with authority and with acknowledging the opinions of others. At social gatherings, you will see him holding forth; when the topic moves on, he will often look for another group that is willing to listen to him. He can be charming and funny; he can also be controlling and critical. Harry came into treatment because he had amassed an enormous credit card debt, which he had hidden from his wife. When she inadvertently opened one of the bills and discovered the extent of the problem, she announced that she had had it with his lying and secretiveness, and was filing for divorce. In addition, although she did not know it yet, Harry's job was in jeopardy owing to "personality differences" with his superiors. He did not understand why his wife was so angry or his colleagues and bosses so intolerant and impossible, but he did not like the way he felt and thought that if he could say he was in therapy, everyone would "get off his case."

Kathy, on the other hand, hungers for approval. She married a molecular biologist who has a good position in the pharmaceutical industry, and spends much of her time managing their home so that it meets his needs. She takes care of the three children and pushes them hard, trying to arrange for their success at school and in sports. She works part-time as the assistant director of a successful nursery school at her church; she takes pleasure in being seen as a small part of a larger whole. She is a perfectionist, and gets upset if she feels she has failed anyone. At the same time, she devotes little time to herself, stating that she prefers to be in the shadow of her husband, children, and superiors. She came into treatment when her husband lost his job and her middle son was acting out in school. Beneath this apparent investment in the object is rage for ruining her "perfect" world.

These two people do not sound alike. One appears invested in himself, and the other in the object. Yet, if we scratch the surface and look at the intrapsychic structures, we see a very different picture.

I. DESCRIPTION

The *Grandiose or Exhibitionistic Narcissistic Disorder:* We are all familiar with the picture of grandiosity. This is Harry. This is the individual with a façade of self-assurance, self-confidence, and self-preoccupation, who constantly pursues admiration. Perfectionistic in striving for money, power, and fame, he shows an extreme sense of entitlement, grows enraged when criticized, and lacks empathy and concern for others in spite of pursuing them to obtain their admiration and approval.

The surface adaptation and lack of anxiety and depression exhibited by many patients with an Exhibitionistic Narcissistic Disorder can be misleading; they often look pretty good and on the outside appear to be functioning well. It is only when something in their world breaks down, often in their jobs or their families, that we see what lies beneath the façade. The underlying feelings include intense envy, rage, feelings of worthlessness and rejection, and a pervasive sense of impotence and inadequacy.

The *Closet Narcissistic Disorder:* The person with a Closet Narcissistic Disorder can be deceiving. He or she does not display overtly exhibitionistic behavior, and may even present as humble, anxious, inhibited, or shy. He or she may often first appear to be a person with a Borderline Personality Disorder in his or her focus on the object. This is so because the major emotional investment of the individual with a Closet Narcissistic Disorder is in the omnipotent other rather than in the self. The other is idealized and the patient's grandiosity is gratified. The patient then "basks in the glow" of the object. These individuals do not have the capacity consistently to maintain the continuity of defense of the Grandiose Narcissistic patient, and are more prone to experiencing envy and self-esteem impairment. They are also more likely to be depressed. Kathy is a good example of a patient with a Closet Narcissistic Disorder. She, as is frequently the case, first appeared to have a more Borderline personality organization. It was only upon examination of her underlying intrapsychic structure and her response to intervention that the similarities with the more overtly Exhibitionist Narcissistic personality became apparent. If treatment of the Closet Narcissistic patient is successful, as many of the defenses against manifest grandiosity are interpreted and resolved, the false grandiose self and its need for mirroring and idealizing will appear more clearly.

The *Devaluing Narcissistic Disorder:* Most patients with a Narcissistic Disorder of the Self will fall into the above two categories, activating a grandiose self or identifying with an omnipotent other. However, a smaller group encompasses patients who are different, either projecting the underlying impaired self onto the other and then acting out the role of the harsh attacking object by devaluing anyone in their path, or by projecting the harsh object and taking on the role of the impaired self. This is the patient who will find fault with everything the therapist does, who is always expecting, and finding, narcissistic injury.

II. DIFFERENTIAL DIAGNOSIS

To arrive at a differential diagnosis, seven factors must be considered (Masterson & Klein, 1989, p. 9):

1. The presenting picture of the false, defensive self.
2. A review of current ego/self functions and impairments.
3. Developmental history.
4. Medical history.
5. Family history.
6. An assessment of intrapsychic structures.
7. The nature of the therapeutic relationship and response to interventions.

Once both psychosis and neurosis have been ruled out, it is necessary to differentiate among the Disorders of the Self. The style of defense in the person with a Narcissistic Personality Disorder differs from that of a person with a Borderline Personality Disorder, where the self- and object-representations are separate and split into two alternating part-units. The Narcissistic patient's self- and object-representations are fused rather than separate. The Borderline patient's projections of the rewarding and withdrawing units are not so strong that reality can be totally denied, devalued, or avoided. There is less access to aggression. In contrast, an Exhibitionistic Narcissistic patient maintains a continuity of self-representation that is seemingly invulnerable, masking the depression beneath. The depression itself is marked by narcissistic outrage, feelings of humiliation, and fear of fragmentation. The rage has a quality of coldness and lacks the relatedness of that of the Borderline patient. The themes of power, perfection, and envy, so prominent in the patient with a Narcissistic Personality Disorder, are minimal in the Borderline patient, whose themes tend to be depression and anger at the loss of wished-for supplies. The Narcissistic personality fears fragmentation of self, whereas the Borderline personality fears loss of the object.

Likewise, the intrapsychic structure of the Schizoid Personality Disorder differs from that of the Narcissistic Personality Disorder in that it consists of two split, defensive object relations units. This patient's seeming narcissism reflects a need to maintain a safe distance from others and a strong desire not to have to rely on anyone, and is not a reflection of an underlying grandiose self-representation. There is a relatedness in the Narcissistic patient's need for mirroring or perfectionistic strivings that is absent in the Schizoid patient, for whom there is no conviction that a communication network is in place, or even possible, without grave risk and danger (Masterson, 1993, Chap. 3). The patient with a Narcissistic Personality Disorder pursues admiration, perfection, and mirroring, whereas the primary goal of the Schizoid patient is safety.

Further, the Exhibitionistic and Closet Narcissistic Disorders can be differentiated from each other by the way in which the patient presents his or her false self — as either inflated (grandiose) or deflated (closet), that is, by whether the primary focus is on the self or on the object.

Diagnosis can be further confirmed by response to treatment, as will be discussed later.

III. DEVELOPMENTAL THEORY

One of the real problems with understanding the Narcissistic Personality Disorder is the seeming paradox that a very primitive self/object-representation is seen alongside what appears to be a high capacity for ego functioning. Dr. Masterson speculates, from his work with adult Narcissistic patients, that the basic arrest precedes that of the Borderline Personality Disorder, that is, that it occurs in what Margaret Mahler has termed the practicing subphase of the separation–individuation process rather than during rapprochement. This is the time when the child starts to crawl, then walk, returning to the mother for "emotional refueling" (quoted in Mahler, Pine, & Bergman, 1976, p. 69). The toddler has a "love affair with the world" (quoted in Mahler, Pine, & Bergman, 1976, p. 70). The chief characteristic at this point is the child's great narcissistic investment in his or her own functioning, body, and the objects and objectives of the child's expanding reality. He or she shows a relatively great imperviousness to bumps and falls.

Typically, the Narcissistic patient, particularly the higher-level one, will describe his or her childhood as good, with idealization of the parents. However, three basic histories emerge.

1. *Exhibitionistic:* Parents use the child as an extension of their own grandiosity. Expectations are projected onto the child, who feels adored, admired, and loved in a way, through this projection. The mother is always there to promote the child. The real self goes underground; the child's grandiose self is being mirrored and stays out. Any appearance of the real self is met with scorn, humiliation, derision, shame, cold

withdrawal, disapproval. In response, the idealized child will bring out parts of the self that connect with the mother, developing into a fused, grandiose, omnipotent unit. The child feels loved, but, in fact, was used. Upon closer examination, the mother appears to have been cold and exploitative, unable to acknowledge, confirm, or support her child's real self, and instead, treats the child as an extension of her own frustrated needs. The child's preoccupation with maintaining the mother's idealization preserves the grandiose self and helps to avoid awareness of the real self and of the mother's empathic failures and depersonification of her child. This is the child who develops an Exhibitionistic Narcissistic Personality Disorder (grandiose self — omnipotent object). (In part from Fischer, in Masterson & Klein, 1989, pp. 70–71.)

Harry's history supports the development of his personality structure. Historically, Harry was an only child born to older parents. His father, a mechanic, was described as unaffectionate, passive, distant, and envious of his son. His mother worked as a nurse. Harry described her as a dependent, fearful, symbiotic, but not nurturing, woman who lived for her son and made him the center of her life. She waited on him hand and foot, and he learned early on to "yes her to death" and tune her out. Harry stated that he has known that he was special and destined for great things since he was quite young, and is sure that if he could only find a job without incompetent management, his inherent abilities would be readily apparent. Meanwhile, he has to tune out the ridiculous things people say to him at work, and "is just as glad" when he is fired, so he can escape an environment that does not allow him to demonstrate his potential. Likewise, in his marriage, Harry reports similar patterns, often tuning his wife out when she is critical and feeling particularly good when she recognizes and comments on his superior abilities.

2. *Closet:* In the second case, there are two possible scenarios. One, the child comes up against subtle or not-so-subtle scorn, derision, and humiliation for expressing her real self. She has memories of being attacked, devalued, and disparaged as a child. She learned not to get rid of the grandiosity, but to put it into hiding. She connected with the parent by downplaying her self, by excessive modesty. She is constantly scanning the environment for evidence of the hostile depreciation by the other. Or, two, the parent communicates to the child that if the child reveres the parent, the child will be loved, adored, and tended to. In either case, the probable outcome is a Closet Narcissistic Personality Disorder, where the child idealizes the parent and effaces the self. This person is more prone to narcissistic vulnerability and injury, and is more aware of the impaired self (Fischer, in Masterson & Klein, 1989, p. 70), and can often first appear to have a Borderline personality structure.

In reporting her history, Kathy noted that she was an only child born after her parents had immigrated to the United States. They apparently had had another child, a son who died at about 9 years of age during World War II. The son was apparently idealized by both parents, and Kathy felt that nothing she did would ever come close to making up that loss. She described her father as ineffectual, sweet, often depressed, never very successful, and somewhat lost. Her mother worked on an assembly line, but would go to work every day dressed in a suit and white gloves. She was experienced as a critical, narcissistic woman whose constantly repeated message to Kathy had been to protect her from any information or emotion that might upset her. Kathy said that her mother loved her best when she was "seen and not heard," but was a good student whose performance reflected well on her parents. She stated that she forever falls short of her mother's (and her own) need for perfection, and repeatedly expressed her sense of her own inadequacy about her ability to function in an autonomous position. She has a paralyzing fear of being a disappointment in her own eyes and those of the other, and demonstrated an inability to observe and take credit for her many accomplishments, saying, "If I can't see myself reflected positively in the eyes of the other person, I have no self."

3. *Devaluing:* Derision moves into intimidation, violence, violation, abuse, a consistent threat against expressing real or grandiose needs. This kind of treatment can result in a low-level Devaluing Narcissistic Disorder. There is no grandiosity of the self or idealization of the other, but the child lives in a state of siege, with paranoid, Schizoid defenses. In treatment, the patient's fragmented self is defended against by projecting either the attacking object or the impaired self onto the therapist. Some of these patients will use the Devaluing defense to maintain a derisive sense of superiority over people in their environments, whereas others will appear to be functioning at a low level, and can often be confused with patients with Schizoid Personality Disorders.

IV. INTRAPSYCHIC STRUCTURE

Understanding and being able to map out the intrapsychic structure of a patient is crucial to making an accurate diagnosis, which then becomes the basis for determining the type of intervention that will be most effective. Unlike the DSM-IV, which presents a purely descriptive, external portrayal of the Narcissistic Personality Disorder, the Masterson Approach utilizes an understanding of the internal intrapsychic structure of the patient.

The person with a Narcissistic personality organization has a fused object relations unit (see chart on page 80), which differs markedly from the split object relations unit of the Borderline patient. In the Narcissistic Personality Disorder, this part of the intrapsychic structure has been designated the "grandiose self–omnipotent other." The outward, defensive unit is that of a grandiose self–object, which is superior and elite, with an affect of being perfect, special, or unique. The omnipotent object is perfect and powerful, and necessary for idealization and mirroring. The Classical or Exhibitionistic Narcissistic person constantly activates this structure with its need for

SPLIT OBJECT RELATIONS UNIT OF THE NARCISSISTIC PERSONALITY DISORDER

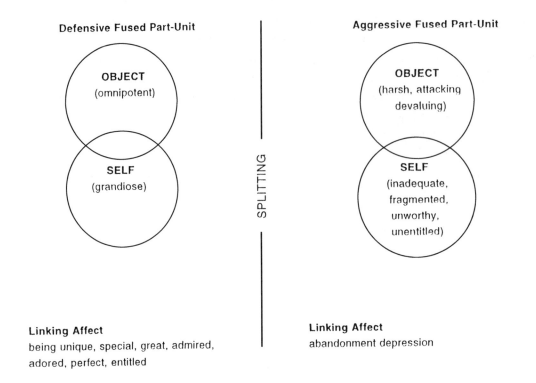

Defensive Fused Part-Unit

OBJECT
(omnipotent)

SELF
(grandiose)

SPLITTING

Aggressive Fused Part-Unit

OBJECT
(harsh, attacking
devaluing)

SELF
(inadequate,
fragmented,
unworthy,
unentitled)

Linking Affect
being unique, special, great, admired,
adored, perfect, entitled

Linking Affect
abandonment depression

Ego Functions — poor reality perception; impulse control; frustration tolerance; ego boundaries.
Ego Defense Mechanism — splitting; avoidance; denial; acting out; clinging, projection; projective
   identification.

grandiose exhibition. Projecting this self, he or she exhibits his or her specialness and expects perfect mirroring of this grandiosity and unique perfection. The Closet Narcissistic patient projects the omnipotent object, and idealizes the perfection of the object, which he or she expects to share, that is, the patient basks in the glow of the object. The linking affect in both cases is one of being unique, great, wonderful, special, promising, adored, perfect, entitled.

What is well hidden beneath this grandiose self–omnipotent object structure is the aggressive or empty object relations unit, which is the other fused self/object-representation. It consists of an object that is harsh, punitive, and attacking and a self-representation that is humiliated, shamed, and empty, linked by the affects of the abandonment depression, which are different from those of the Borderline individual. With the Narcissistic personality, the abandonment depression is experienced as shame, humiliation, narcissistic injury, a colder sense of outrage, and a lack of relatedness. The resulting extreme sensitivity to feeling criticized or attacked forces the therapist to rely on therapeutic interventions other than confrontation, primarily mirroring interpretations of narcissistic vulnerability (Fischer, in Masterson & Klein, 1995, p. 70). The abandonment depression of this unit can be brought on, either by efforts at true self-activation (the pursuit of realistic, self-expressive goals as opposed to the narcissistic goals of perfection, money, power, beauty, and so on), or by the perception of the object's failure to provide perfect mirroring.

Because the affects of the abandonment depression are so devastating, they are immediately defended against by externalizing the depression and projecting its object-representation as causing the depression. In other words, the problem is out there; it is what others are doing to the patient that is so upsetting. The patient then proceeds to avoid, deny, and/or devalue the offending other, thereby restoring the balance of his or her narcissistic equilibrium and avoiding the experience of depression. The relatively free access to aggression enables the person with a Narcissistic Personality Disorder either aggressively to coerce the environment into resonating with his or her narcissistic projections, or, if this fails, to deal with that failure by projection, avoidance, denial, and devaluation (Masterson, 1981, p. 16). In order to protect this illusion of omnipotence and invulnerability, the patient will deny, devalue, dismiss, withdraw from, or rationalize any stimuli that challenge this omnipotence and invulnerability.

Therefore, in order to keep his grandiosity intact and the underlying depression at bay, Harry's explanations for his lost jobs and marital problems were that his superiors were basically jerks who did not appreciate his suggestions and ideas, while his wife simply misunderstood him, could not see the wisdom of his choices, and was unsupportive. He was sure that if she could be made to see the error of her ways, all would indeed be well again in the marriage. Kathy, whose husband had lost his job and whose perfect son was acting out in school, could no longer maintain the continuity of her idealizing defense and lapsed into depression. In terms of her intrapsychic structure, this means that she could not stay in the grandiose self–omnipotent object unit, and instead, was subject to the very painful affects of the abandonment depression.

The intrapsychic structure of the child is formed in response to developmental stressors that result from a combination of nature, nurture, and fate. Nature refers to the genetic endowment of the infant, whereas nurture reflects the maternal capacity to support the emerging self. Fate includes factors beyond the control of the family, such as illness, death, war, famine, natural or engineered disasters, and other emergencies that interfere with the mother's capacity and availability for nurturing and support for separation and individuation or with the infant's ability to elicit and make use of maternal supplies. When the sense of self of the Narcissistic patient has been so severely injured because of ruptures in any or all of these, a child will:

1. Dismiss the real self, and try to recapture the narcissistic relationship by becoming grandiose.
2. Push the real self underground, idealize the object, and try to comply (Closet).

3.   Or feel under siege, in danger of disintegration or fragmentation if the object was so narcissistically injurious. The child will give up on being mirrored by, or idealizing, the mother. There is a strong development of the aggressive–empty unit that is projected externally, in order to protect the self against the perception that the other is harsh and attacking (Devaluing).

The resulting impairments in ego functioning will include poor reality testing, poor impulse control, poor frustration tolerance, poor ego boundaries, and the use of aggression to manipulate the external world to get narcissistic supplies. The ego defense mechanisms that will be most prominent are splitting, avoidance, denial, acting out, clinging, projection, projective identification, idealization, externalization, devaluation, and omnipotence.

For the person with a Narcissistic Personality Disorder, self-esteem and self-worth are externally derived. These patients tend to do better earlier in life than later, when losses and demands for intimacy and to give are much stronger. Aging is the ultimate narcissistic wound.

V. TREATMENT

The Narcissistic patient enters treatment with a focus on defense rather than on internal conflict and painful affect. It is only through the appropriate handling of these defenses that the patient gets to the underlying conflict, with its associated painful affect. The main therapeutic challenge when working with the Narcissistic patient becomes finding a way to enter the patient's system to effect therapeutic change without precipitating a defensive reaction. How do you phrase your interventions when anything you say that interrupts the patient's sense of being perfectly mirrored or validated by you is likely to be experienced as an attack or a criticism? What is the language we can use to address the Narcissistic patient, which the patient will be able to hear constructively, and which will promote further exploration rather than trigger defense?

With the Borderline patient, the focus is on confrontation of defense. Confrontation of the Narcissistic patient, however, will be experienced as an attack on the grandiose self, resulting in a real sense of narcissistic injury and necessitating a tightening of defense. It is, therefore, crucial to find a way to speak so that the patient can hear what the therapist is saying.

Therapeutic neutrality and keeping to the therapeutic frame are the anchors of this treatment. The therapist holds to the frame, expecting that the patient will identify his or her feelings and discuss them. Narcissistic patients will avoid pain by avoiding exposure of their real selves, seeking instead something that feels better, either fusion with or idealization of the object. The therapeutic frame and therapeutic neutrality are injuries to the grandiose self. The therapist's job is to hold the frame and neutrality in position and interpret the inevitable narcissistic injury to the patient. The therapist must work hard not to resonate with the patient's wish to be admired or fear of being attacked. The patient's transference acting out serves the purpose of defending against feeling and memory; therefore, in the transference acting out, the patient will unconsciously externalize onto the therapist in the present the problems from the past. The frame will then act as a container for the patient's projections, and for the therapist's countertransference.

The therapeutic task, as with all Disorders of the Self, is to track the triad (self-activation leads to painful affect, which leads to defense), and then to intervene in such a way as to interrupt defense and lead the patient to the underlying affect. Such repeated interventions serve to convert transference acting out to transference and therapeutic alliance, which will establish the beginnings of trust in the relationship and bring to center stage the patient's avoidance of self-activation as a defense against painful affect. Therefore, the therapist will only intervene when the patient is transference acting out, when the fusion fantasy of perfect mirroring is interrupted and the patient is disappointed or angry. With the Grandiose Narcissistic patient, the therapist's focus should be on failures of perfect mirroring of the grandiose self and on defenses. In the case of the Closet Narcissistic patient, the focus should be on the failures in the idealized object. The issue for the therapist, then, is exactly how to articulate the interventions. The vehicle for doing this is called the mirroring interpretation of narcissistic vulnerability. In this intervention, the therapist will mirror, understand, empathize with the pain of the individual, which opens up a patient–therapist experience of fusion, of being on the same page. Then it is possible to add an interpretation of the defensive function of the behavior, to "sneak it in by the back door," so to speak. Interventions are only made when the patient is experiencing a narcissistic injury of some sort, in order first to reestablish a sense of fusion, and only then to add an interpretation.

The mirroring interpretation of narcissistic vulnerability consists of three parts, which can be remembered by the phrase "pain, self, defense." Broken down, each component of the intervention is as follows:

1. **PAIN**: Identify and acknowledge the painful affect the patient's self is feeling. This is the mirror that demonstrates to the patient that you understand and empathize with what he or she is expressing, and makes it possible for you then to add:
2. **SELF**: Emphasize the impact on the patient's self in such a way as to indicate your understanding of the patient's experience.
3. **DEFENSE**: Identify and address the defense or resistance, which can then be

tied to the first part by observing how it protects, defends, calms, and soothes the patient from the experience of the painful affect. It is important to point out the function of the defense with great care in order to avoid precipitating a narcissistic injury. Keep in mind that the patient's action arose from a need to maintain his or her self-esteem or sense of self-cohesion.

The Exhibitionistic Narcissistic Disorder

Most Narcissistic patients come in to get better regulation of their self-esteem; often this results either through fusion with the therapist or in response to the therapist's mirroring. Therefore, the focus of the work will initially be on the here and now in the interactions between patient and therapist. With the patient with grandiose defenses, the therapist interprets the therapist's failure in being perfectly empathic and in perfectly mirroring the patient's grandiose self. Through repeated mirroring interpretations of narcissistic vulnerability, the patient becomes aware of the need for perfect mirroring from the therapist, which can then be generalized. Often Exhibitionistic patients can go on at length, paying little attention to the therapist, secure in their defensive grandiosity that the therapist is enthralled and of one mind with them. Should they touch on a subject that brings up painful affect, they will change the topic to one that moves them away from feeling by reinstating the defense. With an accurate mirroring interpretation of narcissistic vulnerability, the patient, feeling understood by the therapist, can begin to contain some of his or her transference acting out and permit some access to the split-off painful affect. Eventually, the transference acting out becomes more ego-dystonic, leading to the formation of transference and a therapeutic alliance. Without an appropriate intervention, some patients can go on for years without making any significant progress. What keeps them in treatment is the maintenance of the constant activation of the grandiose self–omnipotent object fused unit, enabling them to feel perfectly understood, unique, and special. When an intervention abruptly disrupts the sense of merger, the patient will feel narcissistically wounded, criticized, misunderstood, and badly treated. In that case, the patient will often leave therapy prematurely and abruptly.

Examples

Harry came into session furious at the boss who had recently fired him, labeling the man an "incompetent jerk." He had apparently let the boss know what he thought of him, which had not been well received. He was also not happy with his wife's angry reaction to him, and had verbally attacked her to the point where she kicked him out of the bedroom. I knew from past history that he could easily turn his anger on me, so I said: "You sound infuriated and disappointed with both your ex-boss and your wife (*pain*). You must feel misunderstood, and perhaps rejected, on both fronts (*self*), and the way you could help yourself to feel better was to let your boss and your wife know exactly what you thought of their responses (*defense*)." Harry: "You know, it really hurt when they behaved that way."

Or: Harry reacted quite negatively when I was mistakenly buzzed during his session. He was clearly (and loudly) angry, telling me that I had no right to pick up the phone on his time, that I was supposed to be paying attention to him. I observed: "I think that you must have experienced my picking up the phone as a difficult disruption (*pain*). You were just telling me how you handled that situation with your boss and how annoying his response was. When I picked up the phone, it must have seemed to you as though I thought that what you were saying wasn't important (*self*). Getting angry at me is your way of trying to protect yourself from the painful feelings that this situation brought up" (*defense*). At this point, Harry stopped berating me. He quietly noted that this time, I seemed to have understood what he was feeling. He then spoke with some affect of how difficult it was for him to be interrupted, how he would lose his train of thought and his sense of being in control.

The Closet Narcissistic Disorder

Unlike the Exhibitionistic patient, the less obvious Closet Narcissistic patient's transference acting out will take the form of focusing on the object instead of on his or her own painful feelings. Often this type of defense can be mistaken for the clinging of the Borderline Personality Disorder, and can only be differentiated by understanding the function of the defense. The purpose of an appropriate mirroring interpretation in this case will be to bring this behavior to the patient's attention so as to interrupt transference acting out and allow access to the underlying painful affect.

Examples

Focusing on the Therapist

Often, Kathy would begin her sessions with a statement such as: "I really don't know what to talk about today. Tell me where to start." In order to call her attention to her difficulty in focusing on herself, I might say: "You really don't much like focusing on yourself, especially at the start of the session (*pain*) because when you do, you feel very exposed and vulnerable, as if somehow you will pick the wrong thing to talk about and possibly disappoint me (*self*). To protect yourself from these painful feelings, you'd rather ask me to decide what we should be discussing" (*defense*). At this, she would settle back in her chair, give a rueful grin, and start to talk about how much she preferred that I suggest a topic so she would know she was doing therapy right, because I was, after all, not only an expert, "but probably the best therapist around." Since I wouldn't cooperate, however, she guessed she'd tell me about what she'd been thinking about her son's being like her father. Understanding the patient's need for idealization made it much harder to buy into her projections!

Or: Kathy also avoided focusing on her own feelings by asking about me. She would try to get me talking about current events, my family, or where I bought my clothes. Once I caught on to what she was doing, I would use a mirroring interpretation of narcissistic vulnerability to bring this to her attention: "It's really difficult for you to talk about yourself (*pain*), which leaves you feeling exposed and vulnerable (*self*). To protect yourself, you try to get me talking, and then maybe we can stay away from that painful stuff" (*defense*). She might then acknowledge what I had said and move back to looking at herself, or she might deflect again by talking about someone or something else.

Focusing on the object might also take the form of jealousy or envy of others who are perceived as having something the patient wants, either materially or personally (confidence, admiration, etc.). Often, this envy becomes destructive, ruining relationships and backfiring in an unintended fashion. For example, Kathy would frequently comment about people who stimulated her envy, even as she hung around them, hoping to be part of what she thought of as the "in crowd." She would speak bitterly in therapy about how these people had whatever it was she wanted — money, clothes, the "perfect" spouse, a large house, an important job. Eventually, she would become so angry that she would denigrate the group, move away from them, and start the process all over again with a new group whose perceived perfection first appealed to her, and then aroused her envy. Once I identified the pattern, I could say to her: "Being at that party was really so painful for you because so many of the people there seemed to have so much of what you'd like for yourself (*pain*). When you're with them, all you can think about is what you don't have. Eventually, this causes you to feel terrible about yourself, as though there is something wrong with you (*self*). So, to soothe these feelings, you put the group down and tell yourself that they're not worth it, that you can find better friends (*defense*). The problem is that you can't seem to find a place for yourself."

In addition to mirroring interpretations of narcissistic vulnerability, the therapist can ask the Narcissistic patient clarifying questions that help the patient to put his or her feelings into words, such as: What did it mean to you? How does it affect the way you feel about yourself? How did it feel to tell me about that?

When observing the patient's response to a mirroring interpretations of narcissistic vulnerability, there are some danger signs to look out for. For instance, after giving an appropriate mirroring interpretation that seems to result in a dropping of defense and an experience of painful affect, the patient then misses one or more sessions. Or perhaps the patient might distance in session, that is, repeatedly go into defense when in touch with painful internal states. The risk is that as soon as the patient experiences the therapist as of value, this will evoke dependency feelings that will lead the patient to feeling envy, shame, humiliation, which he or she will then try to control by moving away from treatment. A third example is the patient who does not make use of the therapist's interpretations, and either continuously attacks and devalues the therapist, or acts out in destructive ways out of session.

Understanding the Disorders of the Self Triad is as crucial in working with patients with a Narcissistic Personality Disorder as it is with the other personality disorders. Briefly, what this means is that self-activation leads to anxiety and abandonment depression, which leads to defense. Realistic self-activation ruptures the narcissistic defensive structure, which leads the patient to feeling the painful affects of the abandonment depression. Because the evocation of these feelings is so difficult, the patient goes back into defense. Typically, this takes the form of reinflating the grandiose self, or remobilizing the omnipotent object. The therapist then uses a mirroring interpretation of narcissistic vulnerability to interrupt the defense, and so on. Understanding the operation of the triad allows the therapist to keep silent when the patient is speaking with real affect. When the patient is in defense, the therapist can interpret carefully, so as not to overload the patient's capacity.

With the Exhibitionistic Narcissistic Disorder of the Self, the emphasis is on the interpretation of the patient's vulnerability to narcissistic disappointment of the patient's grandiosity and need for perfection, as seen in the transference acting out (Masterson, 1981, p. 31). For a Closet Narcissist, the emphasis is on interpreting the patient's need to focus on the object.

STAGES OF TREATMENT

There are essentially three stages of treatment in working with a person with a Narcissistic Personality Disorder, as there are with all the personality disorders. The first is the testing phase. During this time, the patient is transference acting out and is exquisitely sensitive to perceived failures of empathy on the part of the therapist. There is little continuity between sessions. As the defenses are gently, but persistently, interrupted through the mirroring interpretations of narcissistic vulnerability, the patient will move into the working-through phase of treatment. At this point, there is the beginning of a therapeutic alliance, but it is still very vulnerable to ruptures until well into the working-through. There is less and less need to use formal interpretations because the patient is transference acting out less often. Gradually, transference acting out is converted into therapeutic alliance and transference. The patient experiences the abandonment depression with its associated affects and memories. He or she has insights about his or her life, and the narcissistic defenses become increasingly ego-alien. The patient spends more time dealing with affect-laden material and the triad recurs with less frequency.

After repeated cycles through the triad, the patient gradually becomes more aware of his or her real self and how it differs from the false, defensive self. As the patient's real self develops, he or she has less need for defensive fusion, the self- and object-representations begin to separate and the abandonment depression emerges as the primary focus of the treatment.

When the abandonment depression has been appropriately addressed, the patient enters the separation stage, where self- and object-representations are now separate and the patient has an integrated, realistic view of himself or herself. The patient is aware of his or her own real needs, wishes, and feelings, and understands the difference between the prior defensive self and the real self. The patient can, and does, activate appropriately. Real intimacy is possible because the patient can experience others as separate individuals with their own separate centers of initiative, which have nothing to do with the patient's defensive needs. The patient no longer needs to fuse with the therapist-object because the patient has a real developed self of his or her own. Naturally, not every Narcissistic patient will continue all the way through the separation stage. In addition to whatever limitations the patient may have, the frequency and cost of the therapy impose their own set of limitations.

SHORTER- VS. LONG-TERM TREATMENT

Shorter-Term Treatment

The basic goal of shorter-term treatment is to improve the patient's adaptation to reality. Because the patient generally comes only once a week and has to maintain his or her defenses to function adaptively the rest of the time, there is built-in difficulty. The therapist cannot expect the patient to give up all defenses, because the therapist will not be there to act as a support. Thus, the therapist has to choose which defenses to interpret and which to leave alone. It is also important to monitor the patient's reactions continually so as not to go further than the patient can tolerate.

Although once-a-week therapy is not enough to allow for a restructuring of the personality, it is enough for the patient to make significant gains in insight and functioning. Through mirroring interpretations, the patient learns that any emotional ups and downs are the result of failures in the patient's defensive fusion. This is an important contribution. Many of these patients come to therapy having no idea why they so frequently feel awful.

In a successful once-a-week therapy, the patient also becomes aware of how his or her defensive acting out has sabotaged his or her own goals. Therefore, the patient accepts the need to behave adaptively in the world, even though he or she still may not want to or totally understand why it is necessary. He or she can gain some control over behaviors and responses in order to adapt more effectively to the reality of the situation, rather than just reacting. There will still be lapses, however, because the basic defensive structure is still in place; the abandonment depression has not been worked through.

Nonetheless, even in once-a-week work, some significant memories are brought up and worked through with affect. To the extent that this happens, some energy is drained from the abandonment depression and the patient feels better and has less need to be defensive.

In general, the successful once-a-week therapy of a patient with a Narcissistic Disorder of the Self allows the patient to get along better with others and to be more realistic about life.

Long-Term Analytic Psychotherapy

Long-term analytic psychotherapy generally means that the patient will have two or more sessions per week. The frequency of the sessions gives those patients who are capable of sustained analytic psychotherapy the opportunity to work through their abandonment depressions, to activate and develop their real selves, and to progress through separation.

COUNTERTRANSFERENCE

Working with Narcissistic patients can arouse intense countertransference feelings in the therapist. The care with which interventions must be made, the exquisite attunement to real and perceived slights to which the therapist must attend, and the frequent narcissistic injury and subsequent anger and sense of being wiped out as a person in the face of the client's projections are some of the more obvious impediments to therapeutic neutrality. Some common countertransference reactions may include fear and tension, a sense of having to walk on eggshells in order to avoid precipitating a narcissistic injury, anger and a desire for retaliation, discomfort with the kind of intense scrutiny that accompanies idealization, the idealization itself, a wish for the patient to terminate treatment, and boredom.

★ ★ ★ ★

In conclusion, let us look at where Harry and Kathy are today. Harry is working again, having found a new job. His wife, after banishing him to the basement for several weeks, decided to take him back. Harry felt good once again, back in control of his life. He assured me that this was the best therapy he had ever had, and he left treatment. As long as his grandiose defense is in place, Harry feels no need for treatment.

Kathy has taken a new job as the director of a very large program, work that is much more in line with her abilities. She has assumed a more visible role at home and in her community. The changes she has made have brought her husband into treatment; both now report (he with some relief!) a more equal and balanced relationship. Kathy is experiencing reduced anxiety and less of a need to be perfect all the time. She has taken up hiking and nature photography, and has turned some of the child-rearing tasks over to her husband. The children are doing well. Kathy says she would like to continue her treatment for a while longer to "solidify" her gains.

7

THE SCHIZOID PERSONALITY DISORDER

Jerry S. Katz, C.S.W.

Mr. C was a 37-year-old gay man who had moved to the East Coast three years earlier. He was employed as a computer programmer, working mostly by himself and preferring a freelance contract so that he could move on to another company at any time. He was short and stocky, and dressed in plain, and sometimes shabby, clothing that made him look colorless and unappealing. At the same time, he had a haughty air, seeming cold and aloof. Mr. C spoke in a drone, slowly, and with a careful choice of words. The only affect he showed was an occasional whining tone when he discussed frustrations.

After several years of living alone, Mr. C had recently allowed a man to move into his apartment. "Joey has a great body, and works out a lot. He is Asian, and doesn't speak much English. At first, since he wanted money after we had sex, I told him to leave. Then he showed up again a few days later, and I took him in."

Mr. C mentioned that Joey had stolen money from him. "I don't trust him; but I don't want him to leave. If we don't have sex for a few days, I fear he won't allow it anymore. I like to be sexually passive, although I'm afraid I'll never be able to be active anymore. I want Joey to be more affectionate, but if he ever tried to kiss me, I'd be horrified; I think I'd lose interest in him and tell him to leave. I just want a stud who will give it to me regularly."

His erotic interest focused mainly on a man's chest hair, which he would often find himself staring at, and which he talked about as though it were separate from the person. He talked about his sexual interests in a clinical, almost dehumanized, manner that somehow also seemed shocking, and possibly violent.

What stood out for me was the contrast between, on the one hand, Mr. C's neutral and aloof presentation, clinical descriptions, and typically isolated work and living choices, and, on the other hand, his desperation about keeping Joey around (seemingly at any cost) and the intensity of his sexual interests. I sensed an intense pathos in Mr. C, which was matched by my own feelings of both repulsion and interest, and also was reflected in his entering therapy just when he seemed to have found someone with whom to live.

In describing himself, Mr. C said, "I don't feel much. Maybe I'm hard-wired differently than others; I wonder if I have emotions. The only emotion I ever feel is a negative one — anger." He described himself as abusing alcohol, although only in the evenings, with several beers. "It fills up a void — I feel less bored — it heightens my sexual feelings; without it, I stalk around the house at night."

His only social contacts were with men who spoke little English, were uneducated, and showed no similar interests. Mr. C voiced complete indifference to forming any nonsexual relationships, saying that there was nothing he would want or get from them, and that his only interest in people was sexual. He said he felt like a complete failure with people. "I can't make it work ... there's no point in trying. So I'm only interested in sex. I give up."

History

Mr. C had no prior history of psychotherapy, and indicated that his ethnic, working-class parents would have shunned it.

The relationship between his parents was a distant one, two people living together but going their separate ways. The distance increased as their marriage went on. Mr. C never witnessed any displays of affection between them, and believed that such displays would have made both of them very uncomfortable.

His mother always became quite anxious if she were to meet new people, and only left the house when she had to. She had never worked, and was suspicious of anyone not in the family. Very possessive of Mr. C's company during his childhood and adolescence, she often manipulated him to stay at home. She would take Mr. C with her when she left the house. As he reached adolescence, other boys teased him about this, but despite his protestations, she continued trying to get him to accompany her.

He experienced her as intrusive and manipulative, and as using him to make her feel less lonely. Mr. C commented that from early in his life "she kept me as her own possession." He felt that his performance of these functions elicited no positive emotional reaction from her, no sense of closeness. In describing his relationship with his mother, he never indicated a positive feeling — only a tone of nonspecific irritation, along with a pervasive sense of feeling plagued.

The father was a salesman who was often away on the road. He was described as distant, and as showing little interest in Mr. C. He showed slightly more interest in the daughter. Mr. C experienced him as withholding of affection toward him. "He favored my sister, and had very little connection with me. If I showed him something

I had made in class, he would barely look up from his TV program." The father avoided discussions that would bring him into conflict with his wife, and Mr. C felt he could not turn to his father as a way of holding off the mother's needs and demands. He said his father had "let me drift into outer space."

The sister was three years younger than Mr. C. Single and barely earning a living, she was described as very withdrawn, isolating herself to the point of being a recluse, involved in solitary hobbies. She and Mr. C had only brief telephone conversations every few months. They rarely visited, even when they lived in the same area.

In early adolescence, Mr. C developed a few friendships with other boys at school, and remembers beginning to be outgoing and to feel popular. His mother reacted by crying and pleading with him not to go on overnight visits to other boys' houses, and by making him feel guilty about any after-school time he spent out of the house. If he threatened to stay out anyway, she would become enraged and begin screaming at him.

As he moved further into adolescence, Mr. C stopped being outgoing and social, and had only acquaintances at school. He began to spend most of his time at home, and directed his interest more to technical devices and gadgets. He became aware of feeling "different" and very isolated.

Mr. C had dreamed of attending a famous technical university in the East. His mother did not want him to move out of the house, so he complied by living at home and attending a nearby college. When he finally moved into his own apartment in his mid-20s, his mother reacted angrily, and his parents would not visit him there. The expectation — which he fulfilled — was that he would visit his parents regularly, and on each visit, perform some task or errand for the mother.

In his 20s, he did have a few limited friendships, but these were relationships in which expressions of affection, commitment, or need were off limits. Any expression by the other person of a wish for closeness would impel Mr. C to distance himself quickly. He described one relationship in which he and the friend enjoyed attending computer conventions and country music shows, occasionally traveling together, and talking about their jobs and other interests. But when this man became depressed and lonely over the loss of his job and asked to spend more time with him, Mr. C responded by refusing, and then ending the relationship.

In his late 20s, Mr. C developed a two-year sexual and domestic relationship with a man who shared some of his interests, seemed genuinely to care about him, and very much wanted the relationship to continue. Mr. C also cared for this man, and struggled to find a way to feel comfortable in the relationship. He described himself as continually anxious around the man, feeling a demand to be with him and to want to be with him, to be affectionate, and to have reciprocal sex. He acknowledged that his partner had not made these demands. His anxiety finally became intolerable, and Mr. C moved out.

The end of this relationship seems to have marked a turning point in Mr. C's struggle to negotiate interpersonal closeness; following this, he kept himself at a much greater distance from others. It is as though he could no longer tolerate the wish to participate in a relationship in which he could emotionally interface with another human being. He now spent most of his evenings and weekends at home alone. At work, he politely refused invitations to socialize with, or even have lunch with, coworkers.

The only type of relationship Mr. C accepted was with men who expected "gifts" after sex, or to be "kept" in his home. During these relationships (each of which lasted a few months), Mr. C would complain about the financial demands, but in those rare instances when the man did not ask for something, Mr. C would himself offer money or a gift. These relationships ended when the man would find someone else.

Mr. C also significantly increased his use of alcohol, drinking every evening and on weekends, beginning as soon as he returned home from work. While he never had blackouts, and was always able to perform his job adequately, the alcohol was used to avoid feelings of boredom and loneliness.

Diagnostic Considerations

Mr. C presented with clear evidence of a personality disorder, in all likelihood, a Schizoid Personality Disorder, since he exhibited a stable and inflexible pattern of withdrawal and detachment from social relationships, present since at least adolescence, which led to distress and impairment. Neither the object nor the self was experienced as containing both good and bad qualities. Objects were seen either as quite dangerous, to be stayed far away from, or as demanding total compliance and the surrender of autonomy. Likewise, the self was experienced either as cast out and unable to obtain human connection, or as having to deny the needs of the self as the price of having that connection.

There were no indications of psychotic thinking, and no history of hospitalization. He had never been on psychoactive medication. Mr. C indicated (the several times I asked about this) that he had not been sexually or physically abused. He may have met DSM-IV criteria for Dysthymic Disorder, although it was difficult to distinguish his characterological hopelessness about connecting, poor self-esteem, and withdrawal tendencies from symptoms of a mood disorder. When I brought up the possibility of medication to treat mood and anxiety, he refused, indicating that it would make him very uncomfortable to ingest a substance that altered his mind in any way. Nevertheless, Mr. C was clearly dependent on alcohol.

Guntrip (1969, pp. 41–44) identified nine characteristics that mark the Schizoid personality. Guntrip's views were elaborated on and incorporated into the Masterson Approach by Ralph Klein, M.D. (Klein, 1993; Masterson & Klein, 1995); this chapter reflects Dr. Klein's contribution. These descriptive clinical manifestations point the way to a diagnosis; however, examination of the intrapsychic structure (see below) is required to confirm it. Although one or two of these manifestations might be present in other personality disorders, most of them would be found in an individual with a Schizoid Personality Disorder. According to Dr. Klein (Masterson & Klein, 1995, p. 23), in order to make the Schizoid diagnosis, it is critical that at least introversion, withdrawnness, and loss of affect be present.

Introversion means that the person is turned inward, in a reliance on the internal world of objects and self for the regulation of psychological functions and affects. The Schizoid individual has an intense inner life (usually very well hidden from view), which includes a great deal of powerful and varied fantasy.

Although largely avoiding social contact and usually alone, Mr. C spent much of his time in fantasy (mainly of a sexual nature) about people. His presenting issues indicated internal preoccupation with connection, desiring, being wanted, and potential rejection and abandonment.

Withdrawnness is detachment from the outer world, and is the opposite side of introversion. For some Schizoid individuals, the withdrawnness can be covert (Dr. Klein refers to these people as Closet Schizoids), hidden behind an engaging and interactive interpersonal style. Here, the person is interacting with others and appears to the observer to be emotionally engaged, yet is emotionally apart, possibly feeling nothing about the interaction.

Mr. C's withdrawnness was clear and pervasive. He spent most of his time alone in his apartment, and showed no interest in relations with others beyond what he considered sexual relationships. Even within these relationships, there was little possibility of verbal communication, let alone shared interests or acknowledgment of affection. While at work, he sometimes joined in office conversation and banter, but he described himself as feeling quite unconnected to, and separate from, others while doing so.

Loss of affect means the state of feeling emotionless, of feeling mechanical and robotlike while relating. Feeling is cut off even while the person seems to be "connecting." This may lead the Schizoid individual to doubt that he or she has feelings at all. Mr. C's questioning as to whether he was capable of feeling, whether he was "hard-wired" differently than others, resulted from his loss of affect around others. Loss of affect occurs more powerfully when the individual is faced with strong affects from others. An example was Mr. C's reaction (cited above) when his lonely and depressed friend asked for a closer relationship. Mr. C experienced himself as "immediately going cold."

Narcissism in this context indicates that the Schizoid individual's emotional investments are within the self; there is little involvement in the actual emotional or psychological world of others. This is not about grandiosity, but about withdrawal of emotional investments from the outer world to the safety of the inner world. Mr. C's profound self-containment resulted from his narcissism; he depended on no one for emotional supplies, but provided these for himself. Also, he related to men in whom he was interested almost exclusively on the basis of the projection onto them, that they were hot studs who wanted nothing other than to be sexual and to use him; it was as though they held no emotional contents of their own.

Self-sufficiency indicates relying solely on oneself. In order to avoid the potential dangers and anxieties associated with relying on others for meeting his or her material or social needs, the person relies only on himself or herself. Mr. C took care of his own material and recreational needs, rejecting all offers from others. In fact, such offers were experienced as threats to his autonomy.

A sense of superiority, or of being better than others in specific ways, may be used by the Schizoid person as a means of keeping apart. This does not result from a grandiose sense of the self, but is instead a rationale for maintaining emotional distance. Although Mr. C felt that his homosexuality was a sign of his own weakness, he also clearly looked down on and scorned other gay men as failed men, and used this as a rationale for avoiding friendships. On those rare occasions when he socialized, it was always with heterosexuals.

Loneliness, which is an inevitable part of being cut off from affective connection with others, is often what inspires the person to come in for treatment. Mr. C did acknowledge his loneliness, but was so frightened by his need for affection that he denied any interest in it.

Depersonalization, a short-term loss of a sense of identity and individuality, is a dissociative defense, with which Schizoid individuals may react to a situation of interpersonal stress that seems overwhelmingly dangerous. It is a more powerful and global reaction than loss of affect. The only situation in which Mr. C reported depersonalization was at business meetings when he had to speak or give a report. He would have the extremely uncomfortable sense of being "outside" of himself.

Regression, as defined by Guntrip, is regression inward and regression backward. Regression inward is to primitive forms of fantasy and self-containment, often of an autoerotic or objectless nature, and can involve preoccupation with body parts. An example was Mr. C's preoccupation with the chest hair of powerful men, which he talked about as though it were a being in itself, separate from the rest of the person. There was also a ritualized, sadomasochistic quality to his sexual interests and acts. Regression backward is to the safety of the womb, the fantasy of protection within a totally safe place, a place without any dangerous connections. Mr. C occasionally talked of wanting to "leave town," of moving somewhere else, to a place where he knew no one and had no connections.

The relation of the descriptive characteristics to each other, and to the Schizoid Personality Disorder, is clarified by looking at the underlying intrapsychic structure.

Intrapsychic Structure

The subjective experience most Schizoid individuals had in their family was different from that of those with other personality disorders. Whereas in the Narcissistic Personality Disorder, the individual receives acknowledgment and affection for mirroring the parent's grandiosity or for living out the idealizing projections of the parent (but not for the child's own developmental needs), and in the Borderline Personality Disorder, the person receives acknowledgment and affection for giving up individuation to take care of the parent and for helping the mother regulate her emotional states, the experience of the Schizoid child was that no matter what he or she did for the parent, there was no genuine and consistent affirmation, affection, or acknowledgment. Efforts to get these emotional supplies were to no avail, and were met with indifference, neglect, or overt or covert sadism. Put another way, there was no discernible "contract" between parents and child that allowed the child a strategy for obtaining emotional connection.

The relations with the parents were usually a one-way street, where the child did things the parents expected or demanded, but the parents would not respond to the child's specific needs. The experience was that of being a dehumanized function that would be asked to serve a purpose, and once that "service" was performed, the child essentially was ignored. Put another way, there was no "contract" between parents and child that allowed the child to achieve a sense of separate but interfaceable minds.

There were no positive relational choices for this child. While persons with other personality disorders have available a mode of relating that can bring a sense of pleasure — albeit at the expense of effective, realistic, and creative living — the Schizoid individual has available only the choice of relating from a very uncomfortable position or of not relating at all. This means that he or she has no interpersonal "feel good" mode.

The developmental history is responsible for the internalized object relations units of the Schizoid Disorder, which have been described by Dr. Klein (Masterson, 1993, p. 41).

Master–Slave Part-Unit

When the Schizoid individual attempts to connect, the master–slave part-unit is activated intrapsychically. The object is perceived as coercive, controlling, manipulating, or appropriating, and the self is perceived as having to conform to these conditions as the price of connection. In order to avoid the alternative of complete psychic isolation, the individual relates, but can only do so on the basis of a false self. According to Masterson (2000, p. 61), "The false self is not based on reality, but on a fantasy, and it maintains self-esteem not by efforts to master reality, but by defending against painful affects." For the Schizoid individual, this means relating is done from the position of a slave.

SPLIT OBJECT RELATIONS UNIT OF THE SCHIZOID DISORDER OF THE SELF

Master Slave Part-Unit		**Sadistic Object — Self-in-Exile Part-Unit**

Part Object-Representation: | **Part Object-Representation:**

 a maternal part-object that is manipulative, coercive, is the master and wants to use, not relate to

 a maternal part-object that is sadistic, dangerous, devaluing depriving, abandoning

(center vertical label: **SPLITTING DEFENSE** *)*

AFFECT

In jail, but connected, existence acknowledged, relief in not being alienated

AFFECT
Abandonment Depression
Depression, rage, loneliness, fear of cosmic aloneness, depair

Part Self Representation: | **Part Self Representation:**

 a part self-representation of a dependent, a slave who provided a function for the object and is a victim

 a part self-representation of being alienated, in exile, isolated but self-contained to self-reliant

Developmental Arrest of the Ego:
Ego Defects — poor reality perception; frustration tolerance; impulse control; ego boundaries.
Primitive Ego Defense Mechanism — splitting; acting out; clinging, avoidance, denial; projection; projective identification, use of fantasy to substitute for real relationships and self-reliance.
Split Ego — reality ego plus pathological (or pleasure) ego.

The affect in this part-unit is of being in jail or imprisoned, of feeling a victim, but also feeling relieved at being allowed some connection with the human world. These representations and affects produce a sense of great ambivalence and pathos, of wanting to connect and, at the same time, wanting to escape.

Mr. C would act out this part-unit when he assumed he had to pay me for sessions that I had canceled due to illness. His projection was that I would expect and demand payment, and that he would have no right to protest or refuse it if he wished to remain in therapy with me.

Both sides of the master–slave part-unit were clear in his relations with the men with whom he was involved. Mr. C felt that he was expected to pay for everything in the relationship or the man would not stay with him, and that he was expected to ask for very little in return besides occasional sex. If no payment were requested, he would supply it anyway. On the other hand, by setting up the relationship in this way Mr. C also managed potential feelings of appropriation by himself, controlling whether and under what circumstances the relationship would take place, and by ensuring that any expressions of affection were avoided or rationalized away.

Sadistic Object/Self-in-Exile Part-Unit

The representations in this part-unit derive from those experiences where the child was treated sadistically, or devalued, deprived, or abandoned when the child sought to relate as more than a function — in other words, when the child attempted self-activation.

In this part-unit, the object is experienced as malevolent and discouraging attempts at connection. The individual distances. The self is experienced as in exile, alienated and isolated, but also thereby protected against the malevolence. Here, the self is in a safe haven where there is no intrusion. But this safety comes only at the enormous price of being cut off from emotional supplies, cut off from being fully human.

The affects in this part-unit are those of the abandonment depression: despair, depression, rage, profound aloneness, terror. Mr. C likely experienced this when he would "stalk around the house, alone at night." Another phrase descriptive of this affective state was, "My father let me float off into outer space." Thus, while the individual feels free, the affects in this unit are so frightening that they motivate attempts at making some connection to others —usually in reality, always in the fantasy life.

The lower-level Schizoid individual predominantly projects the sadistic object/self-in-exile part-unit in the transference acting out and outside of therapy. Here, the parental object has been experienced as so appropriating, manipulative, and potentially rejecting that even attempts to relate in the master–slave unit are fraught with danger. While some Schizoid individuals spend almost all of their time in this unit, such people rarely come into treatment, or they come in a crisis situation and leave as soon as it's over. They may use alcohol or other substances as the only safe way to keep alive the intrapsychic hope for human connection. If life events conspire to make them lose this hope, they may become suicidal. However, most Schizoid patients are not this hopeless and despairing.

Mr. C had the profound belief that others would reject and angrily rebuff any attempts at connection on his part — "not give me the time of day" — and that the malevolence and intensity of the rejection would be in proportion to his own wish for connection; in other words, just because he expressed the wish. Thus, he experienced the very desire for connection as dangerous.

Several times during the first years of his treatment, Mr. C mentioned that he had thought of calling me over the weekend, usually if he was particularly upset about an event in his life. He refrained from doing this because he was certain that while I would respond politely, I would only be "going through the motions," would really find the call an unpleasant annoyance, and would disingenuously find a way to get off the phone as soon as possible.

An example of his most typical and basic experience in relating to others was when he attempted to conduct a conversation with someone. Mr. C felt that he "shriveled up" and was "unable to fulfill my part of the contract" as the conversation progressed, and then he became anxious and needed to break off the interaction. Exploration of this experience led to his belief that others demanded a response from him, that he was expected to speak in a "nice" way and have a great deal to say, and that failing this, the other person would be quite angry and have no further interest in relating to him. The simple wish to converse with others opened him up to the dangers of coercion, appropriation, and rejection.

Therapeutic Stance, Interventions, and Course of Therapy

Within the therapeutic relationship, the Schizoid Disorders of the Self Triad consists of the transference acting out of various forms of distancing as a defense against the anxiety and abandonment depression evoked by the push to connect with the therapist. This distancing can make it seem as though the patient has little or no affective connection to the therapist, an appearance responsible for the idea that Schizoid patients have no wish to relate. This is rarely the case; almost all Schizoid patients — except those Schizoid individuals who have lost all hope — keep open the conscious or unconscious wish for and motivation toward emotional connection with other humans. The therapist must view the patient's distancing as transference acting out — a defensive action — rather than as a neurologic deficiency or a simple preference. Particularly with a lower-level Schizoid patient, the therapist must work to maintain and proceed from the assumption — sometimes in the absence of obvious clinical confirmation, and against the patient's verbalizations that he or she is "hard-wired" that way or just does not care about relating — that the patient retains the hope, and indeed the longing, for closeness although terrified of acknowledging it. The patient's remaining in treatment is a silent indication that the patient has a "private" (in the fantasy life) connection with the therapist, which is of critical importance to the patient.

During the first years of once-a-week treatment Mr. C primarily transference acted out the sadistic object/self-in-exile unit. He alternately projected the sadistic object onto me and responded, for example, by showing no affect, sometimes not responding at all to my verbalizations, by maintaining that my only interest in him was financial. Alternately, he assumed the sadistic role and made me feel in exile (projective identification) by speaking in a flat, droning voice, paying for sessions with an air of annoyance, maintaining he was getting nothing out of therapy and threatening to end it, telling me I meant nothing to him and describing his sexual activities in a cold and provocative manner, as if throwing them in my face.

My countertransference reactions corresponded to his projection of these units. It was quite a challenge for me to overcome feelings that Mr. C was "hopeless," "just a maintenance case," whom I should refer elsewhere (my assuming the sadistic object role), or feeling frustrated and angry, endlessly "plagued" and "stuck" with him, useless, without impact or value, and then detached and withdrawn (my accepting the self-in-exile position).

The therapeutic interventions used to convert the transference acting out of other patients with personality disorders into transference and to establish a therapeutic alliance with them are usually experienced as controlling or appropriating by the Schizoid patient. Confrontation, which helps the Borderline patient recognize and then control the denied maladaptive consequences of his or her behavior, is experienced by the Schizoid as an attempt to coerce the patient to act in a certain way, to push the therapist-master's agenda and force the patient to surrender his or her autonomy. Mirroring Interpretations of Narcissistic Vulnerability, in which mirroring of the Narcissist's pain opens a door to exploration of defenses against that pain, seems like an intrusive attempt by the therapist to insinuate himself or herself into the Schizoid patient's "head," and thereby appropriate or take over that patient's thoughts and feelings for the therapist's benefit.

In hoping to deal with his distancing (and, no doubt, also countertransference acting out my own feeling of being in exile by trying to lure him closer to me), I several times made mirroring interpretations of Mr. C's anxiety about potentially connecting to me. I said, "It makes you so uncomfortable to want to feel closer to me that you distance from me in order to soothe your anxiety." I believe he immediately sensed my need for confirmation of an emotional bond between us; Schizoid individuals have an enormous sensitivity to such needs, which are experienced as demands. His reaction each time was an immediate further detachment from me, stating that while I was "apparently a nice guy, it wouldn't have any effect on me if I never saw you again." This sadistic response — conveyed also by his cold facial expression and impassive gaze — made me feel as though my office had become very cold, as if I were suddenly locked in a refrigerator.

During this testing phase of treatment, Mr. C was testing whether I would retaliate to his sadism or his withdrawal by pushing him, attacking him, or withdrawing. In other words, he was testing whether he could feel safe with me. Many therapies end up stalemated at this point because the therapist, also longing for greater connection and confirmation, acts out the patient's projections.

Aside from maintaining therapeutic neutrality in the face of these projections, the therapist creates the conditions under which the Schizoid patient can feel safe by indicating his or her understanding of the patient's Schizoid dilemma, which is that "the patient can be neither too close nor too far in emotional distance from another person without experiencing conflict and anxiety. To be too close exposes the patient to the fear of appropriation and manipulation and is unsafe. Yet to be in exile — too far — is to risk the anxiety of unbearable isolation and alienation" (Klein, 1993, p. 44).

Interpretation of the Schizoid dilemma is the primary intervention used to establish a therapeutic alliance with a Schizoid patient. To be effective, this inter-pretation must be made in a way that demonstrates an understanding of the potential dangers facing the patient in taking in what the therapist says. The therapist offers un-derstanding of what may be going on inside the patient that motivates the distancing, and does it in a way that is not categorical, that indicates it is only a possibility that can be rejected (or indeed not even responded to), and makes it clear that this is the therapist's thinking about the topic, which might or might not correspond to how the patient thinks or feels about it. The patient will not feel safe unless the patient believes that the therapist has no therapeutic agenda (including getting the patient closer to people) or other personal stake in anything that he or she thinks, does, or says.

As I became experienced in the Masterson Approach, I began making this inter-pretation of Mr. C's Schizoid dilemma in relating to me: "I had a thought about how you might experience being in this room with me. I would be curious to know if this makes any sense to you. It seems to me that being too close or too far away from me may pose a dilemma for you. Acting on a wish to have a connection with me might leave you open to feeling rejected or coerced or manipulated by me — sort of like a slave who has to do what I want or else have nothing — yet, on the other hand, keep-ing yourself at too great a distance from me might leave you feeling profoundly isolated and cut off."

And in terms of his larger experience of relating to others, I said: "Let me see if I understand correctly what you may be experiencing; please correct me if I'm mistak-en. That when you're talking to or being with people, you feel very unsafe because you feel forced and manipulated to be what they want you to be, and only that. So to pro-tect yourself, you pull far back from them. But, on the other hand, when you're pulled far back and not feeling the danger, it is at the terrible cost of feeling totally isolated and cut off."

Mr. C responded at this point in the therapy by denying any interest in connect-ing with me, indicating that he could see no point or value in it since we were not going to have sex. He said that, as a matter of fact, he could not see any reason why he was continuing in therapy, and often considered terminating. As for relating to others, he maintained that his only interest in people was sexual and so he was only interested in seeking relationships with foreign men who had exciting chest hair (by this time, Joey had moved out and left the country).

(Less severely Schizoid individuals can more safely acknowledge their wish for connection; but in a patient like Mr. C the hope for connection has itself become dan-gerous, and the motivation toward it is often denied. In some individuals, the hope has been extinguished; I was unsure about this with Mr. C for a long time.)

★ ★ ★ ★

These reactions to my interpretations of his Schizoid dilemma indicated that Mr. C was not a candidate for shorter-term treatment. Ralph Klein has described the goals, therapeutic process, and selection criteria for patients with personality disorders who can benefit from shorter-term treatment using the Masterson Approach (Klein, 1989), and specifically for those Schizoid patients who are likely to benefit (Klein, 1995).

The goals of shorter-term treatment with the Schizoid patient are to lessen interpersonal (Schizoid) anxiety, interrupt withdrawal and retreat, and promote interpersonal communication or connection. This treatment does not eliminate those anxieties, since the patient does not work through the developmental arrest that maintains the split-object relations unit of the Schizoid intrapsychic structure. However, the ability to contain, and then manage, these anxieties allows for more fulfillment and better adaptation to the intrapsychic and interpersonal pressures facing the individual.

The first step in achieving these goals is consensus matching, wherein patient and therapist come to a mutual acknowledgment of the patient's Schizoid anxieties, and the patient feels decreased danger based on knowing that the therapist will provide conditions of safety. The therapist must make early and consistent interpretations of the Schizoid dilemma, which is always present both within the treatment situation and outside of it, and maintain therapeutic neutrality.

The therapist then promotes containment of the patient's wishes defensively to withdraw or distance. The therapist avoids stepping into the patient's projections of enslavement or exile, consistently identifies the patient's movements toward retreat from the therapist and others, and interprets the many Schizoid compromises (see below) the patient uses to stay in a safe position.

Finally, the therapist encourages moves to Schizoid compromises that place the patient progressively closer to others. The idea is conveyed that in order to achieve the patient's goal (not the therapist's!) of closer connection, anxiety is inevitable yet manageable, and action and acceptance of risks are necessary.

The patient's motivation for change, both internal and external, is the most critical predictor of success in shorter-term treatment. For the Schizoid patient, internal motivation refers to dissatisfaction with a previously safe amount of intrapsychic and interpersonal distance; the patient experiences a strong need to move toward closer connection. External motivation results from challenges in the interpersonal environment that put pressure on the patient to move closer to others — a job that requires more intense connection with coworkers or a spouse's move toward increased closeness.

In shorter-term treatment, the Schizoid individual uses the therapist "as a participant in a potential, new object relations unit, one that stands in a realistic, healthy place between the master–slave and the sadistic object/self-in-exile units" (Klein, 1995, p. 121).

Mr. C denied having an interest in a closer connection with me, or with anyone else. On the contrary, he explicitly stated that his only interest in other human beings was sexual. Also, my merely bringing up the topic of his relationship to me had elicited greatly increased distancing, to the point of his suggesting that he might terminate therapy. It was clear that his profound and chronic distancing was ego-syntonic behavior, and that risk taking to achieve greater closeness was currently neither desired nor possible for him. More critically, in terms of his appropriateness for shorter-term treatment, he did not at this time experience me as safe enough to risk positioning me somewhere between master and sadistic object, and himself somewhere between slave and self-in-exile. An extended first step in treatment would be needed, whose goal would be to make it possible for him to take that risk.

★ ★ ★ ★

As I continued offering these interpretations, Mr. C came to react by remaining silent for some minutes. During this silence, however, I would not sense the angry distancing on his part, nor would I feel myself thrust into exile and into the chill I described above.

Over time, Mr. C began to indicate that my interpretations did characterize how he felt in attempting to relate to other people. He gave me information about both sides of his dilemma by discussing in detail his terrific fears of rejection, and by often referring to himself as a very lonely man. He did not risk commenting on this dilemma in relation to me, but instead moved closer to me by revealing his fantasies (which he had only while under the influence of alcohol) of being hugged and kissed by a man. This confirmed a nascent therapeutic alliance.

I then began to interpret the many Schizoid compromises he used to manage his Schizoid dilemma. A Schizoid compromise is a behavior, thought pattern, or relational posture that allows the person to achieve safety by being partly connected and yet partly distanced at the same time. According to Ralph Klein (1993, p. 45), "Linking the patient's efforts at closeness and sharing to defense (distance, self-reliance, or fantasy) through interpretation of the Schizoid compromise interrupts defense and sets the condition for the patient to explore the pathogenesis of the split object relations units."

Interpretation of these compromises also allows the individual to understand, perhaps for the first time, that the patient is actively creating distance, and how it is being done; that this distance may not be a "hard-wired" condition of the psyche; and that moving closer to others may be an option. The patient's understanding of this increases hope.

Having relationships exclusively with men who did not speak his language and shared none of his interests, and seeking relationships where payment was expected, were among Mr. C's Schizoid compromises. So was his desperately seeking to have a man live with him, while abhorring any signs of affection from him.

I said to him, "You've made it clear how lonely you feel. I notice that you seek relationships where only your sexual needs are met, and where you choose to pay the man in various ways. I wonder if your anxieties about becoming too close to someone lead you to settle for relationships where you can be close through sexual connection, but can feel safe by creating distance in all other ways."

After an extended period of such interpretations, Mr. C began to discuss thinking about wanting to move closer to people. Beginning to touch on his abandonment depression, he complained — in a sad, moaning tone — that he felt "suspended between a rock and a hard place." He described feeling tension, anxiety, helplessness, and hopelessness about making any changes in his life. I interpreted these affects of the abandonment depression in terms of the Schizoid triad: that his increasing longing for affection and his movement (still mostly in fantasy) toward people brought up powerful fears of appropriation and rejection, which he defended against by keeping the wishes purely in his head and making no efforts to meet people.

Mr. C then established a closer compromise by inviting another Asian immigrant who had exciting chest hair to move into his home, but one who spoke better English and seemed to enjoy spending time and holding conversations with him. Mr. C would sometimes ask this man to touch him affectionately and enjoyed it when he did. On the other hand, the man denied being gay (although they occasionally had sex), considered Mr. C only a "roommate," and expected Mr. C to pay for his room and board. Affection was never discussed, nor was any possible future for the relationship. Mr. C would complain to me that he wanted more signs of physical affection from the man, and was always afraid he would suddenly disappear, but would never discuss his wishes with him.

On a few occasions, I made interpretations of Mr. C's transference acting out of a Schizoid compromise in relating to me. For example, I said, "You've been coming here for several years. Yet I notice that if I indicate you might feel some connection to me, you withdraw and deny any motivation to be here. I wonder if you might actually want to feel a connection with me, but that acknowledging it would feel too close and too dangerous. So perhaps you make a compromise that lets you feel safe by coming here regularly, but, at the same time, saying that you're not really interested and might leave at any time."

He typically responded with a cold silence, eventually going on to another topic. I did not take up this avoidance, concluding that his connection to me did indeed feel too important and, therefore, too dangerous for him to discuss. As time went on and I noted with pleasure that he was risking closer compromise with others, I told myself that eventually his progress outside of therapy would make me seem a less dangerous object to him, and that we could then work on his transference acting out.

On many occasions throughout the therapy, I told Mr. C that his use of alcohol would inhibit, or possibly preclude, therapeutic progress since he used it to avoid dealing with people. Early in therapy, he acknowledged that this was true, but said he needed his drinking since it was the only thing he looked forward to in life. He later told me he was only able to evoke fantasies of romantic connection after several beers.

All Schizoid persons use fantasy as their most basic Schizoid compromise. Since it allows relating to occur without any taking of risks, it is a substitute for experience and, therefore, a pervasive obstacle to therapeutic progress. Mr. C went a step further and used his relationship with alcohol as a substitute for experience, one that he was unwilling (and possibly unable) to give up for a very long time. About two years after he started therapy, Mr. C developed type II diabetes (adult onset), and became frightened enough of the effects on his blood sugar to stop drinking. But after three months, he resumed, saying he missed his "fun time" too much.

Then, after making his first closer Schizoid compromises, Mr. C used another crisis in his diabetes to stop drinking, but this time has maintained sobriety for (so far) over two years. Having risked moving somewhat closer to others and finding himself feeling sufficiently safe, he could now risk closer compromise in his fantasy life as well. He could now have fantasies about being with men in an affectionate way without the use of alcohol. This critical change, in turn, created the momentum for more risk taking.

I interpreted that his relationship with this second man was a closer Schizoid compromise, one in which he was permitting more affection, conversation, and shared interests, but was maintaining safety by enacting the master–slave unit in paying the bills and avoiding acknowledgment of affection and commitment.

When this man found another relationship, Mr. C was left feeling quite rejected and again doubted that there was any way he could connect with people. Nevertheless, he lost weight, grew a moustache, and spent much money on improving his wardrobe.

Within six months, he had established a third somewhat closer relationship. Although Mr. C was still giving money and gifts, and there was no discussion of a future between them, a good deal of affection was expressed physically, and even verbally, on both sides. Mr. C would let this man kiss him. The sex was more mutual, and he was able to ask the man to admire and stimulate several parts of his body. They enjoyed going many places together. For the first time, he was spending much of his free time out of his house.

He began regularly attending a gay political club, initiating and maintaining conversations with familiar members at each meeting. He invited three of these people to have dinner with him, men to whom he was not sexually attracted. However, the fact that none of these people had returned his invitations left him feeling that no one could like him.

Around this time, Mr. C began occasionally to report dreams in which he was being expelled from a place, or was being pursued and was fleeing. I told him I thought these dreams represented the dangers (sadistic object) he feared as he became more aware of his longing for affection and as he moved toward trying to find it (self-activation). Recently, he has begun noting that these dreams are a "plague" that falls upon him, and he links their occurrence to times he enjoys being with people or talks about personal concerns and interests.

In the past year, he often gave small gifts (e.g., computer software samples) to people in his political organization or to coworkers. He saw this as connecting to people, and felt he was doing "good deeds." When I asked why he felt he needed to give things to people in order to connect with them, he bristled and tried to make me feel guilty for questioning the motive behind this behavior.

A therapeutic alliance is in place when the patient and therapist have reached a consensus that the patient faces the Schizoid dilemma in all aspects of the patient's object relations, including that with the therapist. Despite Mr. C's growing ability to discuss his Schizoid dilemma in relation to others and to make use of this by moving closer to people, a therapeutic alliance had not been firmly established. He continued transference acting out by distancing, avoiding discussion of his wishes for and fears about closeness to me. I was also concerned about his continued acting out of the slave role in relationships by paying and offering gifts. I began to wonder if his unwillingness to discuss his relationship with me was somehow related to his transference acting out in this unit.

A recent incident shed much light on this. I was surprised when Mr. C came in with a gift of software for me. I felt great resistance to refusing it, but was able to pause, and then understand that he was exerting a subtle, yet very powerful, demand that I accept. This was expressed through his seemingly shy and sweet smile, and gestures that indicated that I was being offered something wonderful that I would surely want; it was like an offer from a politician. I immediately flashed to the "friendly" smile with which he had been greeting me over the last months, which had made me slightly uncomfortable, but which I had chosen to accept as his being affectionate with me.

When I stumblingly indicated that I did not feel comfortable accepting the software, Mr. C looked shocked, and then profoundly hurt. He exclaimed, "I can't believe it! How could you treat me so cruelly? I can't believe you would be so callous. Don't you have any mercy?"

After I recovered from feeling cruel and that I absolutely owed it to him to accept his gift and not disappoint him, I was able to explore what this meant to him. He had long believed that, since no one else seemed to like him, at least I was always available to do so. It became clear that he experienced his relationship with me as a kind of refuge, as a safe place to "live" away from the terrors of the rest of the human world. In a way, I was his "one and only." And a condition of his keeping this connection with me was that he be required to give gifts, play the slave role — and that I be required to accept them. My refusing the software was thus experienced as a profound betrayal of this "contract."

This fantasy about our relationship had never been mentioned before, and had been silently guarded in his head for years. It was clearly a critical Schizoid compromise for him, which promoted resistance by allowing him to avoid taking the risk of moving closer to others who might show him even less "mercy." I wondered how it had been enacted between us.

As I thought about this later, I remembered his having given me a gift of software years earlier. Although I had never accepted a gift from a patient before, I had accepted this one because I felt too guilty and frightened of losing him to refuse. I had deflected these countertransference feelings of being enslaved by him by rationalizing that I was helping him to risk closeness with me. Instead, I countertransference acted out the master role by accepting "payment" beyond his fee for the therapeutic relationship.

I noted that he had "forced" me to accept his gift by manipulating me through the demand that I not separate from him, by his seeming helplessness, by his near-rage, and by a kind of simpering salesmanship. He had appropriated me in the same ways his mother had appropriated him.

It now became clear to me that only by interrupting this defense through interpretations of his Schizoid compromises in his relationship with me would I provide the conditions under which he could experience, and then look at, the enormous danger of appropriation and attack that I represent for him. His ability to discuss this danger consistently will indicate that a therapeutic alliance is firmly in place.

I have begun to notice more instances of Mr. C's transference acting out the slave or master role with me, and to bring these up for exploration when he does. For example, now when he greets me with an exaggerated smile and a big hello, I do not smile back (I nod). I ask him if his eagerness to be with me and discuss his personal concerns makes him feel he must pay the price of showing himself in a "pleasant" and exaggeratedly happy way.

When I have interrupted defense in this way, several times at the following session, he would bring in a deeply unsettling nightmare of being violently attacked or chased. I have begun to interpret these dreams as examples of the "plague" he experiences as the price for relating to me without transference acting out the slave role, in other words, when he self-activates.

Mr. C so far has made some important reparative changes in his life and in his overall functioning and his growing ability to make Schizoid compromises that bring him closer to people. However, his abandonment depression remains in place, and with it, his Schizoid intrapsychic structure and impaired real self.

Only by facing his abandonment depression in its full intensity and working it through would he be free of the need to make Schizoid compromises. Working through would involve Mr. C in slowly remembering with feeling the conditions that brought about his need to make these compromises, the dire conditions that were imposed on him by his parents when he attempted to connect with them. He would come to the painful realization that he had no choice in his early efforts to activate his real self, that his only option was to cut off much feeling and knowledge of himself. Mr. C would have to go through the slow and painful process of mourning and grieving this terrible loss. He would then understand and feel the basic need of his real self for affection, empathy, and love from other human beings. His real self would be freed to self-activate in the creative pursuit of these needs.

8

TRAUMA IN BORDERLINE PERSONALITY DISORDERS

Candace Orcutt, Ph.D.

The Borderline Personality Disorder is sometimes thought to originate in early psychic trauma (Van der Kolk, McFarlane, & Weisaeth, 1996, pp. 201–202). But, according to the Masterson Approach, when trauma occurs during the developmental years, its effects are separate from the disorder, and the treatment is different. Often the trauma is hidden behind the Borderline Personality Disorder, and emerges as the disorder is largely resolved. The treatment then must focus on the trauma until that, in turn, is resolved and the vestiges of the disorder again take center stage. (My work with personality disorders over the past 20 years indicates that the Borderline Personality Disorder can exist without early trauma, or that early trauma may be comorbid with other forms of the personality disorder.)

Mrs. V, whose case is described here (with identifying data disguised), presented as suffering from Borderline Personality Disorder, but as the case progressed, early trauma came into focus. It was necessary to shift interventions in order to access and deal with the traumatic material.

CASE ILLUSTRATION

Mrs. V entered therapy with a presenting problem of marital crisis. She and Mr. V had lived together harmoniously for two years, but the marriage of eight months had not gone well. Although they showed each other affection, their sexual relationship had become distant as their commitment to each other had increased. Mrs. V was coming to the painful realization that the problem was mainly hers. She and her husband had tried marital therapy and a brief course of sex therapy: The husband had been non-defensive and understanding, whereas she had continued to pull away, and so she sought individual treatment to try to find a solution.

Mrs. V was 3 years old when her mother died. She had had a chronic cardiac condition, and as a result, had withdrawn from her daughter. The father's attention was absorbed by his work. The situation had seemed to improve just before the mother's death, leaving the patient with a subtle conviction that hope preceded disappointment.

Although Mrs. V's later childhood was often lonely (her father was distracted by work issues), she spent weekends with grandparents who coddled her. This led to another subliminal assumption that good behavior (during the week) would lead to reward (on the weekend).

Mrs. V had dropped out of high school in her senior year — partying was more appealing to her than graduating. She spent her remaining teens and early 20s living at home, working at a series of temporary jobs, and leading a flirtatious social life punctuated by brief liaisons. When she was in her 20s her father died, and she began to live with Mr. V. She came to individual therapy when she was 24.

Mrs. V still looked very much like a teenager. She wore her strawberry blonde hair in a pony tail, and watched the world through lively, somewhat alarmed, green eyes. She was slender, and invariably dressed in tight jeans and colorful tops. She often wore sneakers, but sometimes wore sling-back sandals with small heels. Her mannerisms were nervous and hesitant, and communicated an appealing helplessness.

"I just don't understand it," she said tearfully. "My life had just settled down when it all came apart."

She and her husband had spent their first two years together going to parties, and spending their earnings on eating out and renting time-shares in cabins on the lake in the summer and on the ski slopes in the winter. In a way, she had reclaimed her childhood: working during the week and playing on the weekend.

Their love life had been satisfying during their first years; it had a playful, affectionate quality. But once they settled into marriage, a sense of seriousness seemed to take her pleasure away. She would set out a romantic dinner, with candles and their favorite food ordered in. She would be animated and seductive, until they went to bed. Foreplay would stop as she would suddenly lose interest and pull away, leaving them both frustrated.

She said: "It's bad. We both are starting to look for excitement outside the marriage. We want things to work, but they don't. And I think it's all my fault, but I can't help it."

I asked her what was going on "outside the marriage." She told me she was going to bars and flirting with men there. How far did it go? Only flirting, so it wasn't really so bad.

"You say it isn't so bad, but you also say it's breaking the boundaries of your marriage."

"It's true. I'm fooling myself."

She had reacted positively to confrontation (placing two sides of a split perception in juxtaposition). This helped to confirm a diagnosis of Borderline Personality Disorder. Her positive response to a "playful" rewarding situation, her withdrawal in the face of serious "adult" challenges, and her acting-out flight into flirtatiousness with other men all reinforced the probability of this diagnosis.

At first, she resisted seeing the connection between her avoidance of intimacy with her husband and her flirtatious behavior with other men. Confrontation would lead to momentary insight, but would not hold.

PATIENT: If I can't find pleasure with my husband, why shouldn't I look for a little fun somewhere else?

THERAPIST: When the problem is at home, why should you expect to find the answer outside? [Confrontation]

PATIENT: But why shouldn't I go to bars if he does?

THERAPIST: Two of you doing it helps the marriage? [Continued confrontation]

PATIENT: I guess I should work on my problem at home more. [Confrontation integrated]

She would see the point, but visit bars again as the pressure of intimacy increased. Finally, the reality of the situation frightened her.

PATIENT: This one guy followed me to my car. He said I was a tease and should pay off. He grabbed me. When I screamed, people came from the bar and he went away. I was really shaken up.

THERAPIST: Sounds pretty frightening. Do you think you could learn something from this? [Appealing to observing ego]

PATIENT: O.K., O.K. I'm playing with fire. I'm making more trouble for myself instead of less. [Learned self-confrontation]

As she tried harder to face her problem at home, her husband also stopped reacting and tried to support her. (She was fortunate that her husband remained essentially loyal.) Her anxiety level rose, and was helped by medication. She tried to face the issues that disturbed her while attempting to stay with her husband.

PATIENT: The more I reach out to him, the more I get this strange, cold, sad feeling. It's also scary. This feeling builds up until I have to pull away from Tom. Then we both feel sick and mad again.

I encouraged her to stay with her feelings — no matter how difficult — and see what came to her mind.

For the next few months, she spoke of her childhood as if given permission to open a forbidden door. She spoke especially of a deep loneliness, of being without a mother and feeling distant from her father. Only the attention and affection of her grandparents gave her feelings of warmth in her early years.

As long as she kept away from bars, she grew closer to her husband physically. However, the beginning of abandonment depression took its turn in affecting their relationship. After several months of her tears and frequently expressed sense of worthlessness, her husband suggested that they try a separation until her mood improved. She was still having difficulty making love as well, and he felt he needed some sexual freedom for a while if they were to continue having a relationship.

She agreed, but took it hard. Her depression increased, and initially she tried to lighten it by going to bars. The old defense had lost its appeal, however. She then turned to alcohol, but found it increased her depression. After that, she began to work overtime at her job, skipping meals and social activities.

Confrontation helped her to curtail these maladaptive behaviors. And because she was beginning to see the uselessness of this defensive activity, she responded to confrontation more readily.

THERAPIST: You say you overwork to distract you from a sense of deprivation, but the overwork deprives you of friends and food. [Confrontation]
PATIENT: Yes. You'd think by now I would just learn to be depressed and get on with my life at the same time. [Integration]

Gradually she cut back on all her defensive activity. She was determined to get her life together. Paradoxically, her anxiety increased as her behavior grew healthier. This culminated in a series of terrifying nightmares that left her shaken and resentful that her efforts had had such a result.

She reported dreams in which she was bound to a huge frozen mass. The more she struggled to free herself, the smaller and thinner she became. She would be about to disappear when she would awaken, drenched with sweat, trembling, and crying. A sense of horror persisted into her waking state, and she would be up much of the night, only returning to bed when dawn lightened her window.

Not only did she stay awake, but she also became increasingly unable to get into her bed. This aversion led to her relocation to the couch, where she slept fitfully between nightmares.

At the same time, she grew ravenously hungry during the night. She started binge eating and gained weight, while she lost sleep.

I began to wonder whether her behaviors might be some acting-out equivalent of past feelings and experiences. As Freud theorized in his work on hysteria, repetitive behaviors may really be "strangulated affects" that can only be released from their cycle when put into words. These affects have their base in traumatic experiences originating in childhood (Breuer & Freud, 1893, p. 17).

We now hypothesize that much traumatic experience is incomplete experience held predominantly in the "behavioral" memory system of the brain. The impact of the trauma is perceived nonverbally and expressed in repetitive behavior, feeling, and sensual impressions; these must find verbal expression and comprehension in the "narrative" memory system. When the verbal is synthesized with the nonverbal, perception of the traumatic experience becomes complete (Brown, Scheflin, & Hammond, 1998, pp. 89–93). When this occurs, an abreaction often takes place, in which the person apparently undergoes the traumatic happening fully for the first time, more or less reacting as if the event were occurring at that moment. The traumatic happening can then be processed as a true conscious memory that slowly fades with time.

Since the behavior involved in personality disorders works in a repetitive pattern similiar to traumatic response, the two may reinforce each other and also be confused with each other. Was it possible that Mrs. V's Borderline withdrawal from her husband was somehow intensified by an avoidant traumatic response dissociated from her conscious memory? Could it be that traumatic symptoms — intrusive feelings and behaviors — were coming to the fore as her Borderline symptoms retreated?

I discussed this with her, and also proposed changing the approach of the therapy to address possible early trauma. She indicated she felt that this might be the right track. She also felt as if the therapy were "stuck" and needed a new direction.

I began by reinforcing her sense of security through the use of relaxation exercises and building a "safe place" with hypnosis. Relaxed and in a trance state, she pictured herself in a sunny meadow, enjoying the perfect picnic with close and trusted friends. She was encouraged to hold on to the feeling of serenity and evoke it whenever she became anxious. She was helped to believe in her capacity to contain and call up a sense of calm to create a psychic center of balance whenever she needed it.

She worked on this ego-strengthening process for several weeks. As she became more focused on her ability to create a sense of calm, she felt she was ready to search for a cause of early trauma.

Her functioning was precarious, but sufficient: she still slept on the couch and often woke with hunger pangs, but she managed to supplement her husband's financial support with earnings from temporary clerical jobs. She had a reassuring group of friends to call upon. Her Borderline behavior was under control. Her symptoms of depression and anxiety were modified by a self strengthened by character work (the lessening of her personality disorder) and hypnotic reinforcement. Antidepressant medication and a minor tranquillizer also helped her to stabilize her moods. This seemed a positive time to attempt to facilitate the emergence of possible traumatic material.

Under hypnosis, she indicated that her anxiety and hunger originated at a time earlier than the age of 5, perhaps age 3. This was the time of her mother's death, a deeply disturbing loss, although not ostensibly a traumatic one.

As the form of the therapy shifted, the language also changed. Confrontation no longer held and reflective or cognitive interventions were more useful.

For instance:

PATIENT: I feel terrible. Maybe I should hit the bars and get buzzed. [In defense]
THERAPIST: You feel bad, but you want to turn to something that has always made you feel worse. [Confrontation]
PATIENT: No. I know what you're saying. But I'm just talking because I don't know what to do. [Confrontation not effective]
THERAPIST: It's hard for you when you feel so miserable. [Reflective listening]
PATIENT: That's right. I feel helpless. Who cares?
THERAPIST: If you were talking to a friend who felt this way, you would feel sympathy. [Cognitive]
PATIENT: O.K. I guess I'm just feeling sorry for myself. I have to go through this. I ask, "Why me?" But I know I have to go through it. [Accepting interventions]

As long as a resurgence of Borderline issues did not require confrontation, we stayed with reflective and cognitive interventions. At the same time, the hypnosis encouraged her to go to deeper levels of recollection.

As she reached a more profound sense of relaxation and safety, she began to tolerate fragments of something frightening. The fear came in the form of momentary physical sensations, images, and mental impressions that recalled her nightmares. She felt cold and weighted down, saw a clear glimpse of her bed and recognized it as her mother's. Then the hunger would begin, along with a terrifying sense of desolation.

She said: "I think I was there when my mother died."

The terror emerged between sessions, catching her at times of reverie, as well as at night. She was caught in a painful place: too far advanced to go back, but almost too overwhelmed to proceed.

She became convinced that she was struggling to piece together a memory of lying next to her mother. Except that she was cold, not warm. But why was she so hungry, and where was her father?

When a patient tries to recall traumatic experiences of early childhood, it is especially important, sometimes critical, to find an older adult who can confirm events, or at least provide missing pieces.

Fortunately, Mrs. V remembered a neighbor, who was close to the family during her childhood, and was able to clarify her situation. At first, the neighbor was reluctant to speak. Mrs. V finally told her about her treatment, and her distress. The neighbor then told her that her father had been at a convention when her mother died. The mother, despite her chronic cardiac condition, had been feeling better. The father, overly detached as usual, had left the mother and daughter alone and had gone to the meeting. While he was away, the mother apparently had died in her sleep, leaving her 3-year-old child unattended. The father returned two days later to find his wife dead and his daughter lying next to her. The child had found bread to eat in the kitchen, but was hungry, dehydrated, and apathetic. After a night in the hospital, the child was returned home and, except for the fact of her mother's untimely death, the episode was never mentioned.

"But why not?" Mrs. V asked her neighbor. "Why keep it a secret?"

"Your father thought it was best, since you didn't seem to remember. He wanted it all forgotten."

I confirmed Mrs. V's impression that traumatic experiences and family secrecy often combine to suppress the trauma further.

As for her reaction, Mrs. V now had a coherent impression of lying next to the cold body of her mother, and experiencing terrible physical and emotional hunger. As the impression intensified, so did the feelings, and Mrs. V was unable to work or function more than minimally for a few weeks. She wept for her mother and for herself, and felt immobilized by sorrow and horror.

After the resolution of her past experience, it became clear that Mrs. V had suffered from early childhood Posttraumatic Stress Disorder (PTSD). Her reactions matched the criteria for the disorder outlined in the DSM-IV (American Psychiatric Association, 1994, pp. 427–429).

1. Exposure to the actual death of another, as well as to a threat to herself.
2. Responding with intense fear and helplessness.
3. Persistent reexperiencing of the event in images and perceptions, in her dreams and her actions, and through exposure to external cues that resembled an aspect of the traumatic event, as well as physiological reactivity to the same cues.
4. Persistent avoidance of associated stimuli (generalization of the trauma to relations with her husband).
5. Persistent symptoms of increased arousal, such as sleep disturbance.
6. Chronic PTSD, which continued for more than three months past the traumatic event.

For most of her life, these symptoms had remained obscured by her Borderline Personality Disorder, or entwined with it.

★ ★ ★ ★

After several weeks, the dynamic began to shift. She questioned not only why her father had kept the early episode a secret from her, but also why he had left her and her mother alone in the first place. She was finally able to begin a mourning process.

"He knew she was seriously ill. He knew anything could have happened!" Her anger grew as she thought of her mother's dying alone, and of her own perilous state, and she thought of the father's detached attitude toward her over the years.

"He was so distant when I needed to be loved. And maybe that secret he kept made him more distant. And now he's dead, too, and I can never have this out with him."

Her forthright expression of anger cleared the air and energized her. Then the anger, in turn, gave way to tears. In time, these subsided and she began to return to her daily responsibilities.

In the fourth year of her treatment, Mrs. V reunited with her husband. They were wary of each other, but had always stayed in touch, and still hoped to restore and heal their relationship.

Her fears of intimacy were still there, but in a new form. Now she was reminded of terror more than she actually relived it. And as the feeling became more removed from the present, it began to fade, as well. Slowly, the two started to rebuild their life together.

In the fifth year of the therapy, only occasional nightmares reminded Mrs. V of her early trauma. Her major focus was on the residue of her Borderline Personality Disorder. It was difficult for her to hold steady in her relationship, and she felt the pressure to visit bars again. Confrontation came back into use, although she had learned to confront herself much of the time, and took responsibility for the work. Consciousness was steadily taking the place of impulse, and bringing clarity where shapeless fears had once predominated.

9

COUNTERTRANSFERENCE TO PATIENTS WITH PERSONALITY DISORDERS AND TRAUMA

Steven K. Reed, Ph.D.

I. COUNTERTRANSFERENCE AND TREATMENT

A. Role of Countertransference: A Nuisance or a Tool for Understanding?

If the goal of psychotherapy with Disorders of the Self is to empower the real self and to decrease the false defensive self by working through the abandonment depression and modifying the maladaptive defenses, then one of the most useful therapeutic tools is countertransference. The term "countertransference" has been given various definitions. For my purpose here, one broad definition of countertransference is "all those emotions in the therapist that interfere with the ability to provide a therapeutically neutral frame" for the patient (Masterson, 1993). Countertransference works as a tool that helps the therapist to discern exactly with whom he or she is interacting, the real self or false self of the patient, and what meaning or function this interaction is having for therapy.

For example, Mr. W, a 45-year-old man, was referred for chronic depression. In the initial stage of treatment, he began to talk to me about his recent inpatient hospitalization. Mr. W boasted that within a week of being in the hospital, he had become somewhat of a self-appointed guru. He was giving other patients brilliant tips on how to manage their depression and their anxiety, and he even had some staff members beginning to listen to him. As he was telling me this, going on and on about it, I found myself bored and distracted, and yet pulled into a mirroring trance to pretend that I was interested, listening attentively, and even feeling a pressure to provide a smiling nod. The session ended with my feeling that the interaction with Mr. W was more a nuisance than instructive.

He came to the next session angry and disappointed. When I asked him why, he said that he was disappointed in me because he had fooled me. He had taken my ostensible smile as evidence that he was smarter than I because I couldn't see through his façade, just as he had fooled the patients at the hospital. If so, how could I help him? I had fallen from being a hero (omnipotent object) to a zero (empty self) with that one smile. He then talked about how this façade was a cover-up for his profound sense of being defective to the core. As I began to acknowledge his inner pain (the impaired real self), he commented, "When I get people to admire my performance, it's like cotton candy — sweet but empty, versus when my real pain gets acknowledged, it's like broccoli — it nourishes my body." This is an example of how my countertransference helped to reveal how active his false self was as a cover-up for his impaired real self. Also, it illustrated how powerfully seductive it was for me to resonate with him.

The task of learning with whom we are interacting, whether it be the real self or the false self, is complicated in that the patients themselves are often not aware of the difference, especially in the beginning stages of therapy. An example of this was Ms. D, a Closet Narcissist with whom I felt treatment was going along "perfectly," until I saw a brief look of disappointment when I coughed during one of her sessions. I vaguely sensed that disappointment, but paid little attention to it until it grew into an angry hopelessness. I asked her about her reaction, and apparently one of her idealized fantasies about me, being younger and healthier than she was (she has chronic asthma), was that if I could help her get better emotionally, she would then be invulnerable to her asthma. As she said: "I want to be like Superman — impervious to diseases, including my asthma." My coughing ruptured her idealization of me, leaving me feeling ashamed for having a sore throat. I knew that feeling was really shame that she was projecting onto me because it was too painful for her to contain. This awareness led me to mirror her shame of narcissistic vulnerability. I said, "I sense that your disappointment in my humanness reflects how unacceptable and shameful it is for you to have any imperfection in yourself, even if it's a physical weakness. However, you're in good company because even Superman has a physical vulnerability, Kryptonite." This is an example of where countertransference can become a tool for understanding the internal experience of the patient and the complex multilayered interactions that often take place between us and our patients.

B. Therapist's Awareness of Countertransference

Both of these examples show how challenging it is to hold on to our real selves. In an average day, I may be co-opted, devalued, exiled, made to feel guilty, detached, enslaved, or appropriated a number of times. Holding on to the real self is one of the biggest challenges we have to face as therapists. As a result, I ask myself, hopefully several times during each session, just how connected I am to my real self in the moment. When I do this, my personal sense (and it varies from therapist to therapist) is that I am in my real self when I am feeling emotionally present in the moment, free to be spontaneously creative and objectively compassionate. I sometimes will take a few minutes before the beginning of the day and reflect on the patients I will see. I then ask myself: Of these patients, which ones am I struggling the most with counter-transferentially? Which ones do I dread the most? Which ones do I look forward to the most? And with which ones do I just coast?

These are cues that may help to identify countertransference. The questions help me to focus on the importance of being connected with my real self, and also to acknowledge how easy it is to lose or compromise my real self. This is true for both patients and therapists. In the Masterson Approach, the therapeutic concept of the Disorders of the Self Triad acts like a compass for the therapist trying to hold on to his or her objectivity and real self in the midst of a patient's projections and volatile emotions. The triad (self-activation leads to abandonment depression, which leads to defense) allows the therapist to predict the kind of projections and the corresponding projective identification countertransferences that will arise.

For example, in my work with Mr. W, his narcissistic need for me to mirror his grandiosity can lead me to predict with a fair degree of confidence that, in the ensuing sessions, I will continue to feel this pressure to be invisible and empty, and to mirror with a smile. Anticipating this helps to protect my therapeutic objectivity and my real self. The Disorders of the Self Triad helps to decode object relations theory into user-friendly language that is akin to what Microsoft Windows is to computer theory. This triad provides the pathway for the therapist to track down where the patient's projections are coming from, and what function they are serving, by identifying the split-part object relation units that are operating.

C. Learning the Four-Step Dance of the Split-Part Object Relation Units

The four-step dance refers to the vacillation that occurs between patient and therapist when the patient is identifying with one of the four part object relation units or quadrants and projecting another onto the therapist. For example, in Mr. W's triad, his point of self-activation was to focus on his imperfection, which then led to painful vulnerability (abandonment depression), and then to defenses of idealization and devaluation. His experience of this painful vulnerability was flowing out of the underlying aggressive object/empty self object relation unit. Therefore, when Mr. W began to feel his pain (empty self part unit/quadrant 4), he would then feel that I was judging and laughing at him as he began to project the aggressive object part unit onto me (quadrant 3). Tracking the triad clearly helps to pinpoint precisely which quadrant the patient is camped in, and allows the therapist to hypothesize as to which quadrant the patient is putting the therapist in. The next question then is: After I know what quadrants I am dancing in, what function are these projections serving?

Four Functions of Projective Identification:
Connect, Communicate, Control, and Contain (CCCC)

Projective identification, which can be described briefly as the therapist's identifying with the projections of the patient, serves four potential functions in the interactive dance between patient and therapist. These interactions are often multilayered and complex.

1. Connect. It's a way for the patient to connect with the therapist.
2. Communicate. It's a way for the patient to communicate his or her inner experience to the therapist. This experience often is a window into how patients experienced the original attachments between them and their caregivers.
3. Control. It's a way for the patient to control the reality of the therapist by keeping the therapist frozen in a specific role. It prevents real attachment.
4. Contain. It helps the patient to contain the abandonment depression intrapsychically by externalizing it onto the therapist.

D. A Clinical Example of Predicting Countertransference

Ms. L, a Devaluing Narcissist two years into treatment, originally had come in for anxiety. Her main role in life was shifting from being a homemaker to working at a college administration job, where her performance anxiety and sense of inadequacy were increasing. As treatment progressed, she began to work through her abandonment depression and to separate intrapsychically. As she started to get into her abandonment depression, she began to experience quadrant 4, her empty self. She would then defend against feeling empty and sad by idealizing me (at this point, I asked myself: What quadrant am I in if she is idealizing me? I am in quadrant 1, omnipotent object, and she is in quadrant 2, idealizing self). At the next session, she would tell me how she had been thinking about me. About how understanding and kind I was, and how those positive feelings would help to pull her out of her emptiness. But her idealization of me would last only two sessions before she would begin to devalue me, as well as the treatment, claiming that she was becoming too dependent on me, and that perhaps it was time to quit.

During this dance, I could predict her going from the empty self (quadrant 4) to the idealizing self (quadrant 2), and then quickly to the aggressive object (quadrant 3) as she devalued me. Being able to track her movements gave me some warning of my own countertransference. For example, when she idealized me, I would begin to feel anxious and cautious in response to her syrupy idealization, sensing that I was being set up for the function of containing her empty self, knowing that when her emptiness would bleed through her idealization of me, she would then devalue me. When I "forgot" to track my real self and my countertransference, I would find myself acting it out by being much more directive, mirroring, and, of course, smiling with interest, as with

Mr. W, as a way to maintain her idealization of me in order to avoid her shaming devaluations. I noticed that when she devalued me, my countertransference was one of withdrawing and becoming silent. My withdrawal had more to do with my own personal countertransference than with projective identification. Painfully, I was confronted with my own vulnerabilities and there was no getting away from it. It is at a point like this that I feel grateful that I am a therapist because no other profession focuses on knowing others so intimately while forcing one to grow oneself. Patients such as Ms. L provide a window into our real selves as therapists and gauge how many threads, pockets, or even reservoirs, of abandonment issues we have.

My challenge for the moment with Ms. L was to ask myself: Will I be able to hold on to my real self in the face of her shaming devaluations? Although I was tempted to fantasize about Ms. L's walking out of my office and never returning, I focused instead on holding on to my real self while experiencing the shame that was being dumped on me, reminding myself that to truly understand Ms. L's inner world and her object relation units required me to experience them to some degree before I intervened.

II. DUAL ROLES OF A THERAPIST:
BOUNDARY CONFUSION

A. Character and Trauma Work

Holding on to one's real self is even more difficult with a patient with a Disorder of the Self and a history of traumatic abuse and PTSD. In the psychotherapy that involves both character and trauma work, the therapist has two roles to perform simultaneously, and sometimes antithetically. In maintaining a balance between therapeutic neutrality and therapeutic supportiveness, the character work is based on the therapist's taking a neutral stance to facilitate separation and individuation in the patient. This neutrality communicates the assumption that the patient is able to manage and process the painful affects that have prevented the real self from fully activating. Thus, therapeutic neutrality serves as an effective antidote against helpless regressive defenses that create the most frequent countertransference problems and result in the therapist's becoming a rewarding or caretaking object.[1]

On the other hand, the trauma work requires the therapist at times to take a more active supportive stance in order to help the patient contain traumatic affects that have been uncontainable. The affects of the trauma work are often overwhelming for the patient because they involve annihilation anxiety rather than abandonment

---

[1] I would like to extend a special acknowledgment to Dr. Candace Orcutt for her supervision and input with regard to trauma work. Her insights have been invaluable.

anxiety. The overwhelming nature of the traumatic affects can be seen in the patient's primitive defenses, for example, dissociation or abusive reenactment. A supportive stance on the part of the therapist aims at helping the patient contain the traumatic effects.

Active therapeutic support is needed in the areas of safety, self-soothing behavior, and structuring the session. First is safety. The therapist has to give ongoing reassurance in order to create a sense of safety for the patient. The patient has to be reassured that he or she is safe in the office, safe with the therapist, and safe with his or her own traumatic memories and affects. Common fears of being destroyed, lost forever in the black abyss, and going insane need continuous soothing.

Second, the therapist actively helps the patient to discover self-soothing behaviors both in and out of the sessions, which will help to manage the affect. One example of this is a Schizoid patient I saw for five years, with a high level of dissociation and trauma. She was beginning to process memories of sexual abuse by her father, who was violent and sadistic, and yet she was unable to think of the memory because the level of her annihilation anxiety kept her paralyzed. One day, she brought in a jigsaw puzzle that she wanted to use as a way of containing the anxiety. As I learned later, each time after being abused, she would go to her room and work on a jigsaw puzzle, which would help block out the abuse by numbing the pain; in other words, it was her technique for regulating her annihilation anxiety. She resorted to the puzzle for about 12 sessions, but after she had made the transition into the trauma work, she no longer needed it.

The third area in which active therapeutic support is needed is in structuring the session. Often the therapist needs to take a more active role in structuring the use of time in the session. For example, if a patient is going to be abreacting a traumatic memory, the first part of the session should focus on identifying what is going to be abreacted. The middle part would be focused on the actual abreaction, and the last part would allow enough time for processing and containing the affect.

One golden rule to remember is that the character work always precedes the trauma work. The Masterson Approach (Masterson, 1976) states that ego repair precedes the working-through phase, and that the trauma work is essentially the deeper working through of these patients. A common mistake is for the therapist to view the abreactive work as being primarily curative without doing the necessary character work, thereby putting the patient at risk of being flooded by trauma (iatrogenic retraumatization). On the other end of the continuum, to be content with just doing the character work without addressing the trauma work never resolves the core issues. A balance is needed, and when that balance is achieved, the patient is able to be in control of, and safely work through, the trauma without being flooded.

B. Attachment Dilemma: Using the "Self" of the Therapist in the Therapeutic Relationship

The need for the therapist to use his or her "self" to create an attachment and a level of engagement with the patient often becomes proportional to the level of trauma the patient has suffered. This level of engagement is often required to cut through the varying degrees of depersonalization, derealization, and dissociation that patients with trauma exhibit, which range from PTSD to DID (Dissociative Identity Disorder). Part of the dilemma is: How much do we give of ourselves? How do we find the balance between giving too little and giving too much? Recently, I was talking to a colleague who had decided to cut back from a full-time practice to part-time. The reason? He had just had a patient quit treatment after three years of sessions twice a week and was tired of feeling ineffective, disappointed, and rejected by patients in whom he had invested himself, only to have them quit.

Countertransference, the giving of ourselves in a more genuine way, opens us up to loss. If a patient with whom I have been working intensively for a long time abruptly quits, I hope I feel loss. If I don't, then I worry that I am too detached. If I feel too much loss, I then worry about being overly involved. Becoming overly involved with trauma patients is easy to do because the nature of the work elicits closer attachment for two reasons: (1) The more traumatized the patient has been, the more we are dealing simultaneously with an adult and a victimized child (i.e., in treating DID patients, play therapy is often used for child alters), which potentially can create a dual relationship. (2) Attachment that results from experiencing trauma can bond two people very closely, as we have witnessed during natural disasters or war.

However, the intensity of this attachment can put seductive pressure on the therapist to blur boundaries by becoming a substitute parent (i.e., the corrective reparenting movement) for the patient, which colludes with preserving the wish for reunion rather than giving it up. Our primary role is to assist in the intrapsychic separation, therefore, becoming a guardian of the emerging real self rather than a surrogate parent or social friend. Personally, this intensity usually accentuates my countertransferences. Some common reactions for me are an increase in my rescue fantasies, feelings of guilt for causing pain, or feeling engulfed by thinking that I don't have a life beyond my therapy office.

III. THE CASE STUDY OF MS. B AND COUNTERTRANSFERENCES

Ms. B, 45 years old, is married and has four children. Presenting problems were chronic depression and anxiety. Ms. B's family history included one younger brother and the fact that both of her parents were alcoholics. There had been physical abuse of the brother by the father and the mother. Ms. B reported no memories of being involved in the abuse herself, except for having vague images of hands striking her, but with no faces attached to those hands. She also was acutely aware of being terrified of getting too close to her mother. She had gone away to college, and shortly after Ms. B's graduation, her mother died. Ms. B had always felt guilty.

To deal with his grief, her father promptly remarried. The new stepmother, their former next-door neighbor, became emotionally abusive of Ms. B and forbade her husband to have any contact with her. He complied and cut off all contact. Ms. B felt lost and abandoned, and soon got married herself. The marriage has lasted for over 20 years.

Ms. B's mother had a history of several hospitalizations for psychotic breakdowns. Ms. B had difficulty remembering any specifics of her childhood or adolescence. She was in therapy for five years with one therapist, whom she liked, but felt that the therapy had plateaued and was not getting to the core issues that she sensed were there but couldn't articulate. Ms. B presented herself as a polite, eager-to-please individual who seemed to be feeling much more helpless than her superior IQ and two state championships in tennis would indicate.

A. Impatient Impasse: The Invisible Trauma

The treatment of Ms. B at the third-year mark had been going "well" but had reached an impasse, much as her previous therapy had. Therapy was not deepening. She had cleaned up her boundaries with her family, had started taking classes and developing friendships, but there still was this invisible floor that she couldn't get below. I began to feel like a broken record tracking her triad and confronting her helplessness. This stage of being stuck lasted for over a year, with Ms. B becoming increasingly impatient and me feeling increasingly inadequate. She would be able to dip into a level of abandonment feelings for only a brief time before she would detach. Whenever she was able to stay with her feelings, they would foster a level of annihilation anxiety that would be overpowering and paralyzing.

In one session, she recalled a positive memory of her mother's taking her to a store to buy her materials for a handicraft project. The significance of this did not strike me until the next session, to which she came in feeling very detached and helpless. She stated in her typical way: "I didn't want to come this morning. I am blank and frustrated that every session seems to be a struggle for me without my getting anywhere. I feel stuck today, gray and heavy, like the clouds outside." (There's a 10-minute silence. I begin to feel stuck in that familiar sense of her aimlessly drifting in the session without anything on which to focus.)

PATIENT: "I'm stuck today. Don't know what I should do. What's your suggestion?"
THERAPIST: "I notice that when you are attempting to focus on yourself, you give yourself only 10 minutes and then you get impatient with yourself and give up on yourself and turn to me for direction."

PATIENT: "I've tried and I feel stuck. I'm blank. Any suggestions?

THERAPIST: "Why are you asking me for direction when you're more than capable of providing it for yourself?"

PATIENT: "I hate being in this place. I feel like I'm not doing my job here, nor are you, because we're both sitting here. I'm having the gumption to fight with you. I hate being in this place of being stuck and it feels as though you are not helping me, and it makes me feel very anxious."

THERAPIST: "You are right in that it's your job to focus on yourself rather than fight with me." (I begin to feel inadequate, impatient, and distant as I think about my plans for the weekend. My real self has left the room and I'm starting to resonate with quadrant 3, withdrawing object.)

PATIENT: "I feel alone. I'm stuck. You're not providing direction and I feel I need it. I thought there were two people in this room."

This is an example of my acting out my sense of inadequacy by being distant and impatient with Ms. B, thereby creating an impasse. By this time in treatment, I had developed an alliance with her that allowed me to trust Ms. B's awareness of what she needed from me. I began to ask myself: What is the current triad? Where am I in the four-step dance that obviously is being played out between Ms. B and me? With what projections am I identifying and what are their functions? I had the feeling that I was barking up the wrong tree with my confrontations as they were going nowhere. It then struck me that her helplessness might not constitute a character defense needing confrontation, but rather her being frozen in the trauma work. She could be overwhelmed with annihilation anxiety, or as she stated, "be frozen in the invisible trauma and not even know it," thus the reason for her impatient impasse. So I checked out my hypothesis by asking her how connected she felt to herself and to me in the moment. She reported feeling so detached that she didn't feel real and I was like a piece of furniture in the room.

I could then interpret her level of detachment as a yardstick measuring the amount of invisible terror she was feeling and wondered what she, or we, could do to help process enough of the terror to overcome her detachment. Ms. B then related that in the previous session after the positive memory, on her way home, she had an image flash through her mind of her mother's striking her. She was so overwhelmed by this as she was driving that she felt an impulse to drive into a truck or run into a bridge.

I told her, "The piece that feels missing from our discussion today is acknowledging how really terrified you are about focusing on yourself."

Her response was, "I was feeling like a bad child who was feeling stuck and alone and like you were a taskmaster giving up on me. I guess what you're saying is that there might be a reason for my being stuck and you're not being my taskmaster who's just leaving me hanging."

THERAPIST: "Exactly. Acknowledging how terrified you really are allows you potentially to have compassion for yourself for being stuck because it's not really being stuck then. It's needing a bit more time to metabolize enough of the terror in order to feel safe enough to proceed. That understanding also allows me to feel a respect and a compassion for your struggle, different from our interaction where you are the bad child who's stuck and I am this critical taskmaster who is leaving you hanging." (Ms. B is in quadrant 4, abandoned self, and I am in quadrant 3, withdrawing object.)

PATIENT: "I know you are on my side, but emotionally I want you to be my taskmaster. I want you to make me get into my trauma so I have someone to blame, and I think subconsciously to try to make therapy unsafe by biting off too much too soon. If I become flooded by the pain, it will destroy my therapy, and if you are the one who is pushing me into it, then it gives me an excuse for not trusting you."

In this session, if I had stuck to confronting her helpless defense, I would have inadvertently been reinforcing her deeper defense of distancing by becoming the withdrawing object, as Ms. B had hoped. Yet in other situations when patients are truly acting out helplessness, then reassurance and active support reinforce regression. Ms. B is an example of how focusing just on the character work (i.e., defense analysis of helplessness) can be used as a distancing defense against the trauma work. Or, in the opposite way, the trauma work can be used as a flooding defense against the character work. Our countertransference helps to find this complex balance between the two.

B. Hopelessness: Therapist Defeated by Ms. B's Hopelessness

Therapy progressed as Ms. B continued to grieve her way through the abandonment depression. As she did this, her real self began to emerge in brief flashes. With each flash, she would feel hope. However, hope, in any degree, is often traumatizing for patients like her. In a poignant moment in one session, she was exploring her sadness and it began to rain. Raindrops bounced off the office windows and the sound brought up a nostalgic feeling from her childhood of being in her bedroom listening to the rain. She was still, and enjoying the moment. She said to me, "You know, for over four years, you have been asking me what I am feeling in this moment. I never really quite understood, but now I do. This is the first time I have been completely still on the inside and emotionally present with another person."

Almost immediately after Ms. B said that, she became depressed and sad. She became overwhelmed with hopelessness, of just seeing how profoundly her detachment had robbed her of life — 45 years' worth. What had been a breakthrough, a "golden moment" for the real self, was now crushed by a black hopelessness. The next four to six weeks were spent on damage control, containing her acting out in her family relationships. Then the bombshell hit, with her showing up in tears, devastated by the news that her husband wanted to move to Alaska. When she said this, I was stunned. I saw over four years of hard work on both sides being thrown away. I was feeling hurt, abandoned, angry, and profoundly hopeless. My first thought was of the colleague who was tired of managing loss and disappointment and scaled down his practice. My second thought was that I didn't need her. I would just fill those time slots with someone else. And yet, I knew that this was my weak attempt to console or soothe the loss I was feeling. One of my challenges at this point was to stay connected to my feelings of loss and hopelessness in order to discern whether the intensity of my feelings was coming from projective identification, personal countertransference, or my real self.

Over the next several weeks, I noticed clues that I was acting out my helplessness. I wasn't taking as many process notes during the session, nor was I reviewing the notes before the session, and I noticed that I was starting the sessions late. The biggest piece, though, was that I had not inquired or questioned her need to move, but had hopelessly resigned myself to the therapy's ending. I had been defeated temporarily by Ms. B's hopelessness (I was in quadrant 4, abandoned self, along with Ms. B; Heinrich Racker [1968] calls this concordant countertransference). Once I confronted my own acting out and restored my objectivity, I was able to question why she would move before her therapy had been completed and to confront her hopelessness. She had not even thought that that was an option, saying, "You mean my health and recovery are that important? I guess when it comes to fighting for me, it's never been an option. I abandon myself with a hopeless resignation and do what I'm told." She eventually confronted her husband about her need to complete treatment and he complied. Ms. B's hopelessness had made me falter as the guardian of Ms. B's real self.

C. Engulfment: Containing the Flood of Annihilation Anxiety

The primary challenge for the therapist doing trauma work is to help the patient manage the annihilation anxiety. As Ms. B began processing increasing fragments of memories of physical abuse, the level of annihilation anxiety increased, leaving her with anxiety attacks and nausea, and paralyzed with terror. At first, I didn't have any countertransference reaction to her being flooded by the terror. Or so I thought! But, in reality, my lack of countertransference was the countertransference. I was distancing. My distancing was resulting from my feeling anxious about being engulfed by Ms. B. As I contained my own distancing and began to provide additional support to help her manage the trauma work, I felt increasingly anxious about how much she needed from me. I started to have fears of getting overwhelmed and burned out with my large caseload of trauma patients. I would vacillate between feeling detached and having reparenting fantasies, especially when she abreacted memories of childhood abuse, and vomited in my office.

In other words, as my distancing started to be overcome, I became a receptive container for her annihilation anxiety. I found myself worrying about her and the treatment. I was plagued by questions: Has enough character work been done to proceed with the trauma work? Is the therapeutic relationship empowering the real self or colluding with the false self? Is the pace of the trauma work too slow or too fast? Are there clinical signs that she is overheating or is being flooded? What is her main triad? What quadrants are being projected onto me and what is my countertransference?

As it was, the uncertainty and worry about the unknown were a part of what I was holding for Ms. B, the depth of which was illustrated to me one night when I was drifting off to sleep. I flashed on a childhood memory Ms. B had shared that day of being home alone and picking up the phone, to hear the other phone in the house being picked up. This meant only one thing — an intruder was in the home. (Later this evolved into memories of a neighbor who had molested her when she was home alone.) The danger and terror Ms. B felt as an 11-year-old gave me the chills. It reminded me of an Alfred Hitchcock horror movie. Tears came to my eyes as I experienced the terrifying vulnerability of a defenseless child facing a dangerous predator. This made it clear to me that my challenge with Ms. B was to hold the annihilation anxiety without losing my objectivity.

D. Sadism 101: Introduction to Victim Abuser Dyads

One of the deepest layers of working through the trauma is often the sadism of the abuser and the sadism of the self. It is interesting, although not surprising, that sadism is the countertransference that I am the slowest to recognize in myself, as well as in the patient. One example of this was at the end of one session when Ms. B turned to me and said, "There's something I have on my mind that I would like to say."

At this point, I felt a powerful force of anxiety and shame sweep over me, as if my sense of self were being put through a meat grinder. This was even before she said anything. Her affects were already being transmitted to me nonverbally.

PATIENT: "When I first started to see you, in the first three or four sessions, you seemed to be much more hesitant in your speech. You stuttered a bit. Now you're fine, but I wonder if there has been a change in your level of confidence."
I was silent (thinking her question sounded benign, but my inner reaction was one of feeling astonished and violated). My face turned red with embarrassment and I felt myself shrinking under the weight of shame. Fortunately the session was over. The day was Friday, which gave me the weekend to sort through this. I was astonished that she had brought this up, because when I was growing up, I had speech difficulties. It was a childhood source of personal shame, something that had been dormant since high school. It was as though she could scan who I was, locate a vulnerability, and then exploit it. My challenge again was to stay with this feeling of being shamefully violated in order to understand it more fully.

This was hard for me to do because I no longer felt safe with Ms. B. Therefore, I didn't have a desire to process this with her. I played back those last five minutes many times, and I recalled a very brief smile of pleasure on Ms. B's face as she saw me shrinking with shame. That image made me feel even more hurt and mistrustful. As I was experiencing the shame, I began to ask myself once again: What is the dance I am dancing unknowingly and what function is it serving? I then remembered a previous session in which she had felt herself deepening her attachment to me. She felt it was a breakthrough for her to trust someone this deeply. I agreed. She then recalled a memory of being 7 years old, attempting to attach to her mother by asking her to love and hold her. Her mother just laughed at her and beat her into silence while saying, "Who do you think you are? You don't deserve to be loved. You're a bad girl!"

I remembered feeling particularly moved by Ms. B in that session. It felt like another golden moment for her real self. That was only 10 days ago and this was the predictable backlash. As the weekend ended, the most difficult question for me to solve was how much of this should I share with her. Was I prepared to tolerate another round of sadism? How much of my "real self" (my experience of her and my reactions) could I disclose to Ms. B before it overwhelmed her low tolerance of real interaction and pushed her into defense? I knew that this was primarily an abusive reenactment where Ms. B was in quadrant 3, the sadistic object, and I was in quadrant 4, the victimized self. It also felt to me that all four functions of projective identification were being acted out within our interaction. Despite my theoretical understanding, it didn't help me to shake free from the hurt and betrayal I was feeling.

In session, I first asked Ms. B if she had any reactions to our closing five-minute interaction from the prior session, and she said she did not. I wasn't surprised. You can't analyze what gets acted out, so I shared my reaction. I told her, "I found my response perplexing because your question was quite benign, but my reaction was one of feeling shamed and being pushed away. As if it were no longer safe to be close and I felt powerless to stop it. Are you aware of having feelings that would want to make me feel that way, or is it just me?"

Ms. B replied, "I think it's just you." That momentarily sent a fresh surge of shame through me, but I knew I was on the right track, so I persisted. I then said, "It may be, but I continue to feel pushed away by you, as if I am being stonewalled. Somehow I sense it's not so much about you and me in this moment, but maybe a deeper expression of what you experienced when you acknowledged your core needs for love and safe relationships. How you have been treated, like being shamed, pushed away, and stonewalled by your mother — a place you revisited only 10 days ago, I think is being reenacted between you and me."

She responded that she knew what she had been doing all along and then began to turn on herself with self-hatred and self-loathing. It was obvious that she was in defense, but I didn't intervene. I just let her stay in defense as she was shrinking from the weight of shame and self-hatred. I had a feeling of relief as she was punishing herself, glad to get out from under the shame, but realized it was my own form of revenge. It seemed that I had now become the abuser and she the victim. I contained my acting out by reestablishing my therapeutic neutrality by interpreting her shaming of herself, or me, as a protective sidestepping of the real issue: not being loved the way she needed to be by her family.

In conclusion then, countertransference is a valuable tool that needs to be used in order to help us understand the inner world of the patient and the complexities of the therapeutic relationship. By understanding countertransference effectively, it will help guide us through the different stages of therapy, both the character and the trauma work, to facilitate our roles of being guardians of the real self by preserving the balance of not giving too little or too much. Finally, and more personally, in listening to my own countertransference, I hear an invitation to go to a deeper level of experiencing my own inner complexity in relationship to another person with the hope that the end point of therapy will be achieved: authentic and whole interactions between two real selves.

WORKBOOK QUESTIONNAIRE

1. A patient describes the progress she has made in treatment. She feels strong and has been assertive in several different situations. After mentioning each instance of feeling good, she looks sad and is teary. The most likely reason for this behavior is:

   a. The patient is bipolar.
   b. She exhibits the Disorders of the Self Triad.
   c. The patient is trying to conceal her real feelings.

2. Mr. J came to session late, infuriated because he had been pulled over for speeding on his way to his appointment. He was fuming at the police officer, who, he felt, did not recognize or acknowledge that he was a busy and important man who had no time for such nonsense. He had said as much to the officer, who responded by increasing the charge on the ticket, and, consequently, the fine. In this instance, a mirroring interpretation of narcissistic vulnerability might sound like:

   a. What did you expect to happen? After all, you were speeding.
   b. Getting to your session late and risking my possibly being angry with you feels very dangerous, but getting stopped by the officer must have felt equally upsetting. It must seem as though there is no safe solution.
   c. It was really upsetting for you when the officer did not recognize either your importance or the fact that you had to be somewhere. You must have felt demeaned and diminished. To protect yourself from these uncomfortable feelings, you became angry, and perhaps challenged the officer in a way that seems to have backfired.
   d. Those cops are all incompetent jerks anyway.

3. A therapist who has had only four sessions with a patient with a Borderline Disorder of the Self, and who has a history of severe sexual abuse, tries to get the patient to abreact traumatic memories. The patient becomes flooded with trauma and terminates therapy. This could be an example of:

   a. Malingering.
   b. Vicarious traumatization.
   c. Iatrogenic retraumatization.
   d. Undifferentiated empathy.

4. The following is a sign that trauma is attenuating:

   a. A process of mourning begins.
   b. The patient begins to have protective feelings about her father.
   c. The patient begins to realize that she has been loved.

5. As a patient recovers from trauma:

   a. Her memory of the trauma is dissociated.
   b. She learns to live with feelings of fear.
   c. She may be reminded of the trauma, but no longer relives it.

6. A therapist who has been doing character work with a Borderline patient for two years is ready to begin the trauma work. Of what potential problem will the therapist continually have to be aware in the transference?

   a. The confrontations may have to be increased to contain the overwhelming anxiety coming from the trauma.
   b. As the therapist becomes more active and supportive during the trauma work, he or she will need to resume a position of therapeutic neutrality during the character work. Otherwise, the therapist is risking activation of the rewarding object relations unit.
   c. The level of projective identification would likely be more diverse and of greater intensity, thus slowing the therapeutic progress.
   d. The central therapeutic focus shifts from the behavioral functioning to the intrapsychic structures.

7. The therapeutic frame means (indicate all that apply):

    a. Clear policies that surround the business aspects of therapy.
    b. A model of reality.
    c. A ruler against which to measure the patient's transference acting out.
    d. A framed picture of Sigmund Freud.

8. You have been treating a patient with a Disorder of the Self and Posttraumatic Stress Disorder (PTSD) for several years and the patient is starting the trauma work as memories of sadistic abuse begin to emerge. You notice yourself becoming impatient, irritable, and even repulsed by the patient. You might understand your reaction as:

    a. Projective identification; you are resonating with the aggressive object.
    b. Personal countertransference from a triggering of your childhood issues.
    c. Symptomatic of poor frame boundaries.
    d. a and b.
    e. All of the above.

9. What variation in technique does the following dialog represent?

    PATIENT: I feel terrible. Maybe I should hit the bars and get buzzed.
    THERAPIST: You feel bad, but you want to turn to something that has always made you feel worse.
    PATIENT: No, I know what you're saying. But I'm just talking because I don't know what to do.
    THERAPIST: If you were talking to a friend who felt this way, you would feel sympathy.
    PATIENT: O.K. I guess I should cut myself some slack. I have to go through this.

    a. Mirroring Interpretation of Narcissistic Vulnerability replaces confrontation and proves effective.
    b. Confrontation proves ineffective and is replaced with a cognitive intervention that addresses trauma.
    c. Confrontation succeeds when followed by an expression of sympathy.

10. A Borderline patient has made few attempts to find a job and asks the therapist for a reduced fee until she does. She acts helpless, and claims that there are no good jobs around and that she hates to take temporary work. The therapist does not confront her helpless defense and reduces her fee. The therapist is:

    a. Helping the patient to stay in therapy so that she can work on her issues to eventually activate.

    b. Stepping into the rewarding unit and fostering regression and lack of activation.

    c. Providing a safe and empathetic atmosphere where the patient can work at her own pace.

    d. Employing a reparenting model.

11. The most accurate statement regarding the difference between patients suffering from an Axis II disorder and those suffering from an Axis I disorder is:

    a. Patients with Axis I disorders show more mood swings in their symptom picture.

    b. Patients with Axis I disorders need medication; patients with Axis II disorders do not.

    c. Symptoms of patients with Axis II disorders will show more reactivity to dynamic issues.

12. All patients with Disorders of the Self have failed to achieve:

    a. Consistency in their work patterns.

    b. Whole object relations.

    c. A capacity to tolerate frustration.

13. Generally speaking, when a therapist first becomes aware of experiencing projective identification, it is best to:

    a. Do nothing initially, except to observe and experience it as a potential window into understanding the patient's inner world.

    b. Immediately process the reaction with the patient so that it preserves the freedom of the therapist to free-associate.

    c. Do very little, as most projective identifications are a distraction to therapeutic neutrality.

    d. Apply the appropriate therapeutic intervention, as projective identification qualifies as transference acting out.

14. Consistent interpretation of a patient's Schizoid compromises will likely lead the patient to:

    a. Anxiety-free connection to people.

    b. Compromises that permit more closeness.

    c. Avoidance of the Schizoid dilemma.

    d. More solid compromises.

15. Dreams are more common in which stage of treatment?

    a. Contracting.

    b. Testing.

    c. Working through.

    d. Termination.

16. Ms. K said: "I like to put people on pedestals. When I find out that they are flawed, I am devastated." This statement is indicative of:

    a. A distancing Borderline Personality Disorder.

    b. A clinging Borderline Personality Disorder.

    c. An Exhibitionistic Narcissistic Personality Disorder.

    d. A Closet Narcissistic Personality Disorder.

    e. A Schizoid Personality Disorder.

    f. A "Secret Schizoid" Personality Disorder.

17. The role of projective identification in child–parent interactions is:

    a. Uninvolved.

    b. Harmful.

    c. Vital.

    d. Mildly helpful.

18. The patient missed a session and felt that the therapist shouldn't charge him even though he had been informed of the payment policy. The therapist backed down and fell into the projection of:

    a. Rewarding unit.

    b. Empathy.

    c. Withdrawing unit.

    d. Countertransference.

19. The Disorders of the Self Triad is defined as:

   a. Abandonment depression leads to self-activation, which leads to defense.

   b. Self-activation leads to abandonment depression, which leads to defense.

   c. Defense leads to abandonment depression, which leads to self-activation.

20. 6:04 Client calls to reschedule appointment.
   6:11 Client calls to reschedule appointment.
   6:25 Client calls to say he will be 20 minutes late.
   The client is furious with the therapist, who confronts the resistance.
   Which stage best describes this vignette?

   a. Contracting.

   b. Testing.

   c. Working through.

   d. Separation.

21. In order to promote safety for the Schizoid patient, the therapist should:

   a. Consistently tell the patient that this is a safe environment.

   b. Consistently mirror the patient.

   c. Consistently interpret the patient's Schizoid dilemma.

   d. Share all of his or her feelings with the patient.

22. A child whose environment supports his or her grandiosity and affirms his or her superiority, while ignoring his or her individuality and attempts at self-activation, will most likely become an adult who:

   a. Must at all times maintain a safe distance from others whom he or she experiences as coercive and threatening.

   b. Alternately clings to or distances from the object, which is experienced as rewarding or withdrawing.

   c. Idealizes significant others and derives satisfaction from "basking in the glow" of their specialness.

   d. Attempts to coerce the environment into resonating with and supporting his or her claims of superiority and perfection.

23. Often in doing trauma work, using the "self" of the therapist makes sense in engaging and creating an attachment with the patient because:

    a. The degree of engagement is often required to cut through the varying degrees of depersonalization, derealization, and dissociation.
    b. The positive self-esteem of the therapist can model emotional health.
    c. This is not appropriate because it runs the risk of facilitating regression and transference acting out.
    d. None of the above.

24. The neurobiologic center for the self is in:

    a. The brain stem.
    b. The amygdala.
    c. The orbital prefrontal cortex.
    d. The temporal lobe.

25. Linda has a Borderline Personality Disorder. She is very angry and has nothing good to say about her alcoholic father, who was a poor caretaker and provider, and yet when he calls to chat, she only has positive feelings for him. Linda is exhibiting the following defense:

    a. Splitting.
    b. Repression.
    c. Denial.
    d. Avoidance.

26. Splitting is a hallmark of the Borderline Personality Disorder. It is a defense against the abandonment depression. Splitting:

    a. Separates contradictory images of good and bad mother and good and bad self.
    b. Fosters themes of rewarding for clinging and withdrawing for separation.
    c. Is embedded in the intrapsychic structure.
    d. All of the above.

27. Mr. S indicates in his first session that his coworkers believe that he is "arrogant and superior" because he always excels at his work, never asks for help from anyone, does not attend social functions, and in general behaves as if he is "too good to talk to anyone." He says that he has always been this way, and that it has always caused him trouble. In the case of Mr. S, a differential diagnosis needs to be made among the following possibilities:

    a. Borderline Disorder of the Self and Narcissistic Disorder of the Self.
    b. Closet Narcissistic Disorder of the Self and Exhibitionistic Narcissistic Disorder of the Self.
    c. Narcissistic Disorder of the Self and Schizoid Disorder of the Self.

28. The Closet Narcissistic Personality Disorder can be differentiated from the Exhibitionistic Narcissistic Personality Disorder by:

    a. A fear of being appropriated by the other or of being alone in the universe.
    b. A projection of the rewarding or withdrawing units.
    c. A false self that is grandiose or deflated, with primary focus on the self or on the object.
    d. The profession chosen by the patient.

29. The patient begins to experience abandonment depression for the following reason:

    a. She curtails her acting out.
    b. She abstains from sexual relations with her husband.
    c. She begins to throw herself into her work.

30. Bowlby's research was based on:

    a. Studies of the school and social functions of young children.
    b. Studies of normal development in children.
    c. Studies of young children separated from their mothers.
    d. None of the above.

31. As a child, Larry was allowed to stay home from school when he had not done his homework or was unprepared for a test. His mother thought of herself as sensitive and understanding because he was only a child; her mother had done the same for her when she was a child. Larry's mother is demonstrating:

    a. Attunement.
    b. Fusion.
    c. Approval of regressive behavior.
    d. One-mindedness.

32. After her trauma is resolved:

    a. The patient discontinues therapy.
    b. She focuses on the residue of her Borderline Personality Disorder.
    c. She no longer needs confrontation.

33. When Ms. L meets a man, she immediately becomes involved. After one date, she is in a relationship, seeing the man daily and e-mailing him from her office five times a day. The process of getting to know someone through dating doesn't take place. In Masterson's terms, the Borderline individual is manifesting:

    a. Commitment issues.
    b. Co-dependency.
    c. Instant intimacy and clinging.
    d. An adult child of alcoholic response.

34. In making a differential diagnosis, a Closet Narcissistic Disorder of the Self can often be confused with:

    a. An Exhibitionistic Narcissistic Personality Disorder of the Self.
    b. A "Secret Schizoid" Personality Disorder of the Self.
    c. A Borderline Personality Disorder of the Self.
    d. A Psychopathic Personality Disorder of the Self.

35. The patient in Chapter 8 on trauma is diagnosed as Borderline. Which two of the following indicators are NOT relevant to this diagnosis?

   a. Positive response to confrontation.
   b. Grandiose reaction to interpretation.
   c. Cooperative response to a rewarding situation.
   d. Withdrawal in the face of adult challenges.
   e. A deferential attitude toward idealized others.
   f. Acting out flirtatiousness.

36. The abandonment depression that is avoided at all costs by the Borderline patient is composed of the following major affects:

   a. Hopelessness and helplessness.
   b. Emptiness, void, and guilt.
   c. Homicidal rage and suicidal depression.
   d. All of the above.

37. The patient's observation that she always had certain people on whom she relied to "validate" her and that "there's something about these people, I put them on pedestals, they're special, above me. Then I find out they have clay feet. It's extremely devastating," illustrates which of the following?

   a. Clinging associated with the rewarding unit of the Borderline Personality Disorder.
   b. Idealization and devaluation associated with the Closet Narcissistic Disorder.
   c. The Disorders of the Self Triad.

38. "Working through" with a patient with a Disorder of the Self and with one with a Posttraumatic Stress Disorder (PTSD) share the same central feature, which is:

   a. Giving up the wish for reunion.
   b. Increasing affective tolerance.
   c. Depending on the differential diagnosis.
   d. The degree to which the therapist becomes attuned to the patient.

39. Mr. A, who is seeing two very different women, explains himself in this way: "I want to see both of them. I *need* to see both of them. It gives me a sense of safety. Sue really seems to love me, but she comes on strong, and when I'm with her for too long, I feel as though I'm choking. I think I like the idea better than the reality. Barb, on the other hand, can't seem to commit and only seems interested in me when she knows there is someone else. She feels a lot less threatening, but when I'm with her, I often still feel alone." These statements are an expression of:

   a. The Schizoid compromise.
   b. The alternating object relations units of the Borderline.
   c. A search for one-mindedness with an idealized other.
   d. The oedipal triangle.

40. Mr. K stated: "My boss is a real jerk. I make all these great suggestions as to how he could run the office more efficiently, and he just ignores me. And if he hears me discussing my ideas with coworkers, he gets angry. I don't know why he doesn't get it or why he doesn't want to acknowledge how good my ideas are." This is an example of:

   a. A way of defensively distancing from the object in order to preserve a sense of safety.
   b. A rupture in the patient's grandiose sense of entitlement against which he defends to avoid underlying painful affect.
   c. Distancing and differentiating the self from the object to avoid feeling smothered.

41. In treating Disorders of the Self with Posttraumatic Stress Disorders (PTSD), the therapist has to resume what during the character work?

   a. Managing self-soothing behaviors.
   b. Abreacting traumatic memories.
   c. Becoming aware of the false memory syndrome.
   d. Maintaining therapeutic neutrality.

42. Early trauma is often further suppressed by:

   a. False memories.
   b. Family secrecy.
   c. The normal process of forgetting.

43. Stern differs from Mahler on which two of the following?

    a. There are a stimulus barrier and an undifferentiated phase.

    b. The infant is not a co-creator of his or her own development.

    c. The self and regulating objects mature in parallel from the beginning.

    d. Seeing the child as prewired to see the mother as separate cognitively.

44. Masterson refers to the defensive self of the Borderline individual as:

    a. The distorted self.

    b. The external self.

    c. The false self.

    d. a and c.

45. Following a rejection by an idealized friend, the patient's report of a dream in which she was in "an accident, an explosion . . . a sense of structure flying apart and exploding," is best seen as an illustration of:

    a. Borderline regression.

    b. Psychotic disintegration.

    c. Narcissistic fragmentation.

46. A child of parents who expect the child to be an extension of themselves and who consequently do not acknowledge the child's own uniqueness, but expect a perfect reflection of their own specialness, will, quite possibly, develop:

    a. A Schizoid Personality Disorder of the Self.

    b. A Closet Narcissistic Disorder of the Self.

    c. An Exhibitionistic Narcissistic Disorder of the Self.

    d. A Borderline Personality Disorder of the Self.

47. The Masterson Approach is:

    a. A cognitive, behavioral approach.

    b. A subjective, relational approach.

    c. A developmental self and object relations approach.

    d. Based on symptomatology.

48. Mary, a chronically depressed 18-year-old, thinks of herself as ugly, dumb, and klutzy. She generally feels this way after a fight with her mother, whom she describes as controlling and cold. The best description of this is:

   a. Adolescent turmoil.
   b. WORU self- and object-representation.
   c. Bowlby's insecure attachment style.

49. Ms. R stated: "I bend myself into pretzel shapes to be a perfect wife so my husband will love me. I'm afraid that if he knew how awful I really am, he would be gone in a minute." Ms. R is expressing:

   a. The clinging defense of the Borderline.
   b. Fusion with an idealized other.
   c. A means of relating to her husband whereby she is a slave to him as her master in order to avoid a sense of total isolation.
   d. Her description of a successful marriage.

50. Ms. S insisted that her 14-year-old daughter come into treatment, angrily describing the problem as follows: "I do not understand her behavior at all. She has always been such a sweet child, agreeable, smart, in all, a wonderful reflection of my mothering skills. She even looks exactly like me. Now, all of a sudden, she is uncommunicative, angry, won't wear what I pick out for her, and is generally disagreeable. I'm still the same good mother I've always been. What's wrong with her?" Ms. S. is most likely expressing:

   a. Feelings of Narcissistic outrage at the loss of her sense of merger and perfect fusion with her daughter.
   b. Appropriate anger at her daughter for rejecting her mother's choices.
   c. Disappointment with her daughter's age-appropriate steps toward separation and individuation.
   d. Both a and c.

51. The therapist decides to explore for early trauma for the following two reasons:

   a. The patient continues to go to bars.
   b. The patient's Borderline characteristics refuse to attenuate.
   c. The patient's intrusive feelings and avoidant behaviors continue, although her Borderline defenses have been discontinued.
   d. Resolution of feelings of abandonment depression do not resolve continued anxiety.

52. The maternal part object of the withdrawing unit in the patient's Borderline intrapsychic structure:

    a. Rewards regression and clings to the child.
    b. Fuses with the child and perceives the child as an extension of self.
    c. Withdraws, attacks, and is angry at the child's attempts to individuate.

53. Ms. R reported that her mother always withdrew whenever Ms. R tried to tell her something upsetting or disturbing about herself. Ms. R said she learned early on to share only good things with her mother, creating a false impression so that her mother would not withdraw. This dynamic most likely would encourage the development of:

    a. A Closet Narcissistic Disorder characterized by fusion with and idealization of the object.
    b. A Schizoid Personality Disorder, where the patient feels she must serve the object as the condition of relatedness.
    c. A Borderline Personality Disorder, where the activation of the patient's false self is rewarded and the real self is forced to go into hiding.
    d. All of the above.

54. What are the three parts of a mirroring interpretation of narcissistic vulnerability?

    a. Pain/Interpret/Explain.
    b. Pain/Mirror/Defense.
    c. Pain/Self/Defense.
    d. Mirror/Confront/Defense.

55. What is the relationship between early trauma and the Borderline Personality Disorder?

    a. Early trauma creates Borderline Personality Disorder.
    b. The treatment is the same.
    c. The effects of the two are separate.

56. Mr. T began drinking between sessions to mute the feelings that were surfacing in therapy. The therapist confronted his maladaptive behavior. An example of confrontation is:

   a. You say you want to understand yourself better yet, you drink between sessions. How can you work in therapy if you mask your feelings?

   b. It's so painful to focus on yourself that you soothe yourself by masking your feelings with alcohol.

   c. If you continue to drink, you need to join AA.

   d. This is a result of how your parents dealt with their feelings.

57. A therapist working with a Narcissistic patient yawns in one of the sessions and then immediately feels anxious and inadequate. With which object relations part unit is the therapist resonating?

   a. Omnipotent object.

   b. Grandiose self.

   c. Aggressive object.

   d. Empty self.

58. You are treating a patient who is in the midst of abreacting horrific sexual abuse memories and you notice yourself feeling as though you are in a "fog" or are "floating." The patient begins to report similar feelings. This may reflect:

   a. A projective identification process of dissociation.

   b. That the session is naturally ending as the memory is resolved.

   c. The overinvolvement of the therapist, who is taking on affective aspects of the patient's experience.

   d. A point of Narcissistic fusion between the omnipotent other and the grandiose self.

59. Which two of the following characterize the relationship between the self and the ego?

   a. They develop and function in tandem.

   b. They develop and function separately.

   c. Ego is the integration of self role images; self mediates between conscious and unconscious.

   d. Self is the integration of self role images.

60. Termination is a critical test of the treatment. It tests all but the following:

    a.   The repair and strength of the ego.

    b.   The internalization of a new object.

    c.   The independence and creativity of the patient's self.

    d.   The strength of the patient's dependence on the therapist.

61. Following an emotional session in which Ms. R spoke for the first time about the feelings that prompted her binge eating, she forgot her next appointment. This is an example of:

    a.   Therapeutic alliance.

    b.   Transference.

    c.   Transference acting out.

    d.   The operation of the Disorders of the Self Triad.

    e.   a and b.

    f.   c and d.

62. A characteristic form of transference acting out for a Schizoid patient is:

    a.   Clinging to the therapist.

    b.   Insisting on being perfectly understood.

    c.   Idealizing the therapist.

    d.   Emotional withdrawal.

63. Maintaining therapeutic neutrality with a Schizoid patient requires the therapist to make it clear that he or she:

    a.   Stands for the patient's getting closer to others, and nothing else.

    b.   Has no stake in whether or not the patient moves closer to others.

    c.   Has no interest in anything going on inside the patient.

64. Analytic neutrality is not:

    a.   An attempt to create a therapeutic climate.

    b.   An attempt to keep the focus on the patient.

    c.   A way to keep the therapist's behavior from confirming the patient's projection.

    d.   An attempt to lead the patient into self-activation.

65. Ms. R, who has an eating disorder, noted: "When I am hungry, I feel virtuous, good, thinner, in control, and lovable. But when I binge, I know I am an ugly, disgusting, detestable, fat, out-of-control pig whom no one wants to be with." These statements are most likely an expression of:

    a. The patient's use of her eating behaviors to maintain a safe distance from the object, characteristic of the Schizoid patient.

    b. The split object relations unit of the Borderline Personality Disorder (RORU and WORU).

    c. A Narcissistic attempt to achieve perfection in order to avoid shame and humiliation.

    d. A description of a glandular disorder with which the patient struggles.

66. An object relations view of the real self is that it is:

    a. The reality of the patient's self as viewed by others.

    b. The patient's view of the self as reflected in others.

    c. The view of how the self relates to others.

    d. The sum total of the intrapsychic images of the self and its associated object-representation.

67. Ainsworth described which of the following attachment styles?

    a. Secure, insecure (avoidant, resistant, disoriented, disorganized).

    b. Clinging, distancing, detaching.

    c. Healthy, depressed, suspicious.

    d. Anxious, angry, aloof.

68. The therapist told Ms. S: "You appear to be disappointed in me when I don't seem to have all the answers. It is difficult to see me as not being perfect; you want so much for me to do that for you that you discount your own capacities to take care of, and make good choices for, yourself." This intervention is an example of:

    a. An expression of the therapist's countertransference.

    b. A description of the Schizoid dilemma.

    c. A confrontation.

    d. A Mirroring Interpretation of Narcissistic Vulnerability.

69. An isolated Schizoid patient who was a lawyer saw himself as superior to other lawyers, and declined to socialize with them because of his feelings of superiority. This man likely:

    a.   Has a Narcissistic Personality Disorder.

    b.   Has both a Narcissistic and a Schizoid Personality Disorder.

    c.   Uses a Narcissistic defense to protect his sense of safety.

    d.   Has good taste in people, despite his isolation.

70. Ms. K talked about her role in her family: "If I want to be a part of this family and cared about, I have to play this part. I have been very alone all of my life except for this role as mediator in my family." This is an example of:

    a.   "Good enough" parenting.

    b.   The creativity of the real self.

    c.   The false self.

71. A 50-year-old client consistently runs out of money and expects to be bailed out by others. She announces that she cannot pay her therapy bill and is furious when the therapist doesn't accept her excuses. This is a case of:

    a.   Therapeutic alliance.

    b.   Transference acting out.

    c.   Transference.

72. The expression of the Abandonment Depression by the person with a Narcissistic Personality Disorder will include:

    a.   Feelings of shame, humiliation, cold rage, and fear of fragmentation.

    b.   Feelings of depression, rage, loneliness, fear of cosmic aloneness, despair.

    c.   Homicidal rage, suicidal depression, panic, helplessness and hopelessness, emptiness and void, guilt.

    d.   Feeling stuck between a rock and a hard place.

73. Therapeutic supportiveness in trauma work differs from therapeutic neutrality in character work in which of the following areas?

    a. Safety.
    b. Self-soothing behaviors.
    c. Structuring of the sessions.
    d. All of the above.
    e. Only a and b.
    f. Only b and c.

74. The "behavioral" memory system of the brain does NOT:

    a. Hold traumatic experience as incomplete experience.
    b. Process traumatic experience into words.
    c. Perceive the impact of trauma nonverbally.
    d. Express traumatic experience in repetitive behavior.

75. The patient's self-representation is that of being clingy, dependent, childlike, and a caretaker, with the affect of "feeling good." This self-representation is associated with:

    a. Part self-representation of the WORU.
    b. Projection.
    c. Projective identification.
    d. Part self-representation of the RORU.

76. The therapist must avoid being drawn into the rewarding or withdrawing unit of the Borderline patient. The therapist must employ:

    a. Therapeutic neutrality.
    b. A therapeutic stance.
    c. A therapeutic frame.
    d. All of the above.

77. Individuals with Borderline Personality Disorders have not achieved:

    a. Object constancy.
    b. Autonomy.
    c. Whole object relations.
    d. All of the above.

78. The patient's statement, "I was always ashamed of my mother and I always admired my father," can be seen as a good illustration of the defense of:

    a. Splitting.
    b. The Oedipal Conflict.
    c. Projective identification.

79. Early trauma may be difficult to diagnose because:

    a. Its effects attenuate over time.
    b. Its effects may be hidden behind a personality disorder.
    c. It is transformed into a Borderline Personality Disorder.

80. During a session where Mr. L complained incessantly about his wife's lack of understanding of his unique skills in managing their money, the therapist said something that Mr. L heard as support for his wife. He became enraged at the therapist, wondering why he even bothered seeing a female therapist since "women are all alike anyway." This is an example of:

    a. A response to a Narcissistic injury experienced as a result of the therapist's perceived failure to perfectly mirror and support him.
    b. The response (of a Borderline patient) to a perceived lack of approval on the part of the therapist for his efforts to separate and individuate.
    c. A distancing maneuver (of a Schizoid individual) seeking to avoid feeling co-opted by the therapist.

81. Ms. S is an attractive 50-year-old successful businesswoman who dresses very fashionably. Despite the money she earns, Ms. S is often broke, and has to borrow money for rent and food. Her expenditures are excessive and she refuses to budget. This is an example of:

    a. The operation of the pathological/pleasure ego.
    b. The operation of the reality ego.
    c. The false self of the neurotic.

82. In session, the therapist told Ms. S, "Look at what's going on here. I'm pointing things out to you regarding the consequences of your choices and you respond by talking about your girlfriend. Are we in the same room?" This intervention is an example of:

   a. Interpretation.
   b. Mirroring Interpretation of Narcissistic Vulnerability.
   c. Explanation.
   d. Confrontation.

83. Mr. S states: "I need the perfect woman — smart, model-beautiful, rich. I feel whole and complete when I am with this kind of woman; I am someone worthy of respect." The above is an example of:

   a. Narcissistic fusion of a grandiose self with an omnipotent other.
   b. Borderline clinging, activating the RORU, where the patient is rewarded for regressive behavior.
   c. An example of a Schizoid compromise where the patient's condition for relationship is to become a slave to the object's master.
   d. An expression of poor self-esteem.

84. A differential diagnosis among the Disorders of the Self helps the therapist to identify which projective identifications he or she might experience in reaction to the patient by:

   a. Identifying the points of self-activation.
   b. Deciding what frame issues may be tested during the initial testing phase of therapy.
   c. Identifying the specific underlying split object relations units, and thus the affective components of possible projections.
   d. Understanding the defenses and how they can be addressed within the transference.

85. Initial therapeutic work with early trauma does NOT aim:

   a. To relax the patient for further work.
   b. To strengthen the patient's ego.
   c. To probe for early memories.
   d. To use hypnosis to facilitate the therapy.

86. The clinical self can be described as being:

    a.   How the patient views himself or herself.

    b.   Synonymous with identity.

    c.   A combination of the patient's appearance, mood, and activity.

    d.   Self-image, self-representation, and supraordinate self-organization.

87. The center for the self develops from:

    a.   Maternal caretaking alone.

    b.   Genetic forces alone.

    c.   Genetic and maternal influences.

    d.   None of the above.

88. The patient who is transference acting out:

    a.   Is reenacting his or her childhood without awareness.

    b.   Has whole object relations.

    c.   Can notice the difference between his or her feelings and the separate reality of the other.

89. The intrapsychic structure of a Narcissistic patient consists of:

    a.   A rewarding object relations part-unit and a withdrawing object relations part-unit.

    b.   Two split object relations units, one of which relates to the object as a slave to a master, and the other experiences the object as sadistic, the self in exile.

    c.   A fused object relations unit with an outward defensive unit of a grandiose self and omnipotent other, masking an underlying empty–aggressive unit.

90. After several months of working with a Schizoid patient, the therapist began to believe that the case was hopeless, that the patient could make no progress, and thought about transferring the case to a beginner colleague. This therapist was most likely:

    a.   Practicing justified triage and doing what the patient needs.

    b.   Caught up in countertransference and acting out the patient's projection of the sadistic object.

    c.   Maintaining therapeutic neutrality.

91. The patient stated: "My boss is retiring. I was asked to take over for him,. There is no way I want to do that. I'm a *great* second-in-command, but I do not want the responsibility or the visibility that comes with that job." The patient most likely is expressing:

    a. A withdrawing object relations part-unit.
    b. A major emotional investment in an omnipotent other.
    c. A major emotional investment in a grandiose self.
    d. A need to distance from the object to avoid feeling co-opted, appropriated, or enslaved.

92. The following exchange with the Borderline patient represents what technical result?

    > PATIENT: Why shouldn't I go to bars if he does?
    > THERAPIST: Two of you doing it helps the marriage?
    > PATIENT: I guess I should work more on my problem at home.

    a. Interpretation leads to insight.
    b. Questioning consequences helps understanding.
    c. Confrontation reveals and resolves implied conflict.
    d. Mirroring Interpretation of Narcissistic Vulnerability leads to psychic relief.

93. Mahler's research assumed that:

    a. Genetics alone drives development.
    b. The child sees the mother as separate from birth.
    c. The child has to separate from the symbiotic relationship with the mother.
    d. The self emerges in the symbiotic phase.

94. Stern's research assumed that:

    a. The child has to separate from a symbiotic mother.
    b. The child is prewired to see the mother cognitively as separate from him or her.
    c. The child is prewired to see the mother as separate emotionally.
    d. The wiring for separation develops purely genetically.

95. A Borderline patient in treatment comes late to session, claiming that she had too much to do at work and that traffic was bad. The best way to deal with this event is to:

   a. Empathize with the patient's difficulties, thereby establishing rapport.
   b. Interpret how this behavior fits into early childhood patterns.
   c. Confront the patient about her failure to manage her time appropriately so as not to lose something valuable to herself.

96. Sometimes in working with patients suffering from a Disorder of the Self and Posttraumatic Stress Disorder, a therapist experiences a deeper "connection" with the patient than usual because:

   a. The greater the trauma, the more therapeutically diverse our interventions become (for example, treating patients with Dissociative Identity Disorder where play therapy is sometimes used for child alters).
   b. There is a natural bonding experience that comes from experiencing trauma together.
   c. The therapist may become more of a container for projective identifications and primitive affects.
   d. All of the above.

97. The therapeutic alliance grows out of the _____ stage and is more evident in the _____ stage:

   a. Evaluation; Testing.
   b. Testing; Working-through.
   c. Working-through; Separation.

98. Which of the following is the appropriate treatment of a patient with a Narcissistic Personality Disorder of the Self?

   a. Mirroring Clarification of Narcissistic Injury.
   b. Mirroring Interpretation of Narcissistic Vulnerability.
   c. Mirroring Confrontation of Narcissistic Behavior.
   d. Mirroring Interpretation of Narcissistic Injury.

99. A therapist has a pattern of feeling inadequate and anxious with most patients with whom the therapist works. This is indicative of:

 a. Projective identification with only Borderline Disorders of the Self.
 b. Personal countertransference of the therapist.
 c. Pervasive transference acting out.
 d. All of the above.

100. The patient's recollection of the trauma does NOT emerge as follows:

 a. With fragmentary images, physical sensations, and mental impressions.
 b. In a rising sense of terror.
 c. In an increasing sense of resolution and calm.

101. A differential diagnosis of an Exhibitionistic Narcissistic Personality Disorder would include all of the following choices **except**:

 a. A history wherein the parents expected the child to be an extension of their own grandiosity.
 b. A presenting problem that indicates some sort of interruption of a sense of merger with an idealized other in order to feel admired and loved.
 c. Response to Mirroring Interpretations of Narcissistic Vulnerability with the deepening of affect and the emergence of memories.
 d. Response to confrontations with the deepening of affect and the emergence of memories.
 e. Response to confrontations with anger.

102. What is the false self?

 a. The organization and operation of the patient's defenses against separation anxiety and abandonment depression that are used as a guide.
 b. The way the patient consciously presents the self.
 c. The protection of the healthy real self.
 d. The part of the self that comes from the environment.

103. The split-ego structure of the Borderline patient is divided into the reality principle and the pleasure principle. The Borderline patient's split ego is:

    a. More invested in the pleasure principle.
    b. More invested in the reality principle.
    c. Equally invested in both the reality and the pleasure principles.

104. A personality disorder and a traumatic response may reinforce and be confused with each other because:

    a. They have the same origin.
    b. They express themselves in similar repetitive patterns.
    c. They require the same therapeutic approach.

105. One of the distinguishing characteristics of the Disorders of the Self is that they have:

    a. Whole self and object relations.
    b. Split part-self and object relations.
    c. A realistic view of self and others.
    d. Libidinal self-constancy.

106. Which of the following is NOT a symptom of Posttraumatic Stress Disorder?

    a. Reexperiencing the event in images and perceptions, and in dreams and actions.
    b. Reexperiencing the event through exposure to external cues that resemble an aspect of the event.
    c. Borderline Personality Disorder.
    d. Chronicity — symptoms continuing for more than three months after the traumatic event.

107. For the Narcissistic Personality Disorder patient, self-esteem and self-worth:

    a. Are nonexistent.
    b. Result from a sense of internal cohesion.
    c. Are largely dependent on the responses of others.
    d. Depend on parental supplies for regressive, clinging behaviors.
    e. Result from a need to be independent to avoid feeling co-opted and appropriated by the object.

108. Which of the following are capacities of the self?

    a.   Frustration tolerance, mood control, emotional flexibility.

    b.   Commitment, creativity, intimacy, autonomy.

    c.   Mediation between the conscious and the unconscious.

    d.   Maintenance of the energy level, the concentration level, and focus.

109. The developmental forces that spur the growth of self are:

    a.   Genetic.

    b.   Interactions with a caring object.

    c.   The child's pleasure in new sensations and mastery of adaptation.

    d.   All of the above.

110. Ms. C comes into your office and sits silently in the chair. You do not speak, waiting for her to open the session. Finally, she says angrily, "You're the doctor, why don't you ask me a question? My last therapist always helped me to get started." Which description *best* defines the patient's behavior toward the therapist?

    a.   Passive-aggressive behavior.

    b.   Splitting.

    c.   Transference acting out.

111. The "triad" allows the therapist to understand all but one of these situations:

    a.   Regression.

    b.   Depression.

    c.   Blackouts.

    d.   Missed appointments.

112. A therapist who has a full caseload of trauma-based patients notices that he feels burned out, depressed, overreactive, hypervigilant, and anxious in his personal life. This therapist may be exhibiting symptoms countertransferentially of:

    a.   Intellectual confusion over the role of countertransference.

    b.   Chronic fusion with an idealizing Closet Narcissist.

    c.   Vicarious traumatization.

    d.   Being empathically attuned to the patient.

113. Bowlby's research method differed from those of Mahler and Stern in which of the following two ways?

    a. He included other studies of children with problems.
    b. He followed up his study of children.
    c. He used control studies.
    d. He focused on observation of behavior without intrapsychic hypotheses.

114. Mr. Y's presenting problem is a writer's block. In the course of the first session, he describes his father as a "brilliant perfectionist" who always criticized him and who always demanded complete attention from his mother and himself. Although you know you will need more information to complete your diagnosis, your first thought as you listen to this description is to wonder whether Mr. Y might be suffering from:

    a. A Closet Narcissistic Disorder of the Self.
    b. An Oedipal Conflict.
    c. An Exhibitionistic Narcissistic Disorder of the Self.

115. The development of the self occurs through:

    a. Primarily the mother's interaction with the child.
    b. Dyadic attachment interactions between the mother and the child that are stored in the right brain as self- and object-representations with their associated affects.
    c. Biochemical and hormonal input.
    d. The child's interaction with the entire environment.

116. Fantasy is a prime example of a Schizoid individual's:

    a. Schizoid dilemma.
    b. Schizoid compromise.
    c. Unique creativity.
    d. Unusual cognitive capacity for abstracting.

117. A Schizoid patient mentioned for the first time that she had been thinking about the therapist on the day preceding the session. At the next session, the patient had very little to say, and at the end, she said that she wondered why she was in therapy. This sequence most likely illustrates:

a. How unpredictable Schizoid patients can be.

b. That Schizoid individuals do not have any connection with others.

c. The operation of the Disorders of the Self Triad.

d. The beginning of the end.

118. Mahler's style of research was:

a. To review case histories of child disorders.

b. To make intrapsychic hypotheses from observation of normal children's behaviors.

c. To limit her hypotheses to behavior.

d. To compare normal children with child patients.

119. The patient's statement, "I could never see myself as a leading lady; I was a supporting actress," is most likely indicative of:

a. Failure to self-activate associated with Borderline regression.

b. The idealizing response of the Closet Narcissistic Disorder.

c. The need to act out the slave aspect of the master–slave unit of the Schizoid Personality Disorder.

120. According to Dr. Masterson's theories, based on Margaret Mahler's stages in the separation–individuation process, the developmental arrest for a patient with a Narcissistic Personality Disorder probably takes place:

a. During rapprochement.

b. In the symbiotic stage.

c. In the practicing subphase.

d. On the way to object constancy.

121. Distancing and detachment in response to intimacy challenges may be characteristic of:

a. Schizoid individuals.

b. Borderline individuals.

c. Narcissistic individuals.

d. All of the above.

122. If a Schizoid patient offers the therapist a gift, the therapist should:

    a. Accept the gift as a way of allowing the patient to deepen the connection.
    b. Understand this as the patient's wish to show gratitude.
    c. Both a and b.
    d. Recognize this as the patient's testing whether the therapist will resonate with the master projection.

123. A Schizoid man discussed how dangerous it felt for him to try to make friends, and yet, at the same time, how much he dreaded his feelings of isolation and aloneness in his house on weekends. This is an example of:

    a. The Schizoid triad.
    b. The Schizoid dilemma.
    c. The Schizoid compromise.
    d. None of the above.

124. Intrapsychic structure — the part self- and object-representations and their associated affects — are:

    a. The best way to diagnose a Disorder of the Self.
    b. Basically the same for each category of disorder.
    c. Helpful in diagnosing neurotics.

125. Which two describe functions of the real self?

    a. It provides a vehicle for self-activation.
    b. It mediates between the superego and the id.
    c. It provides a vehicle for ego functions and defenses.
    d. It maintains self-esteem and the mastery of reality tasks.

126. The most significant guide to determining the patient's diagnosis is:

    a. The patient's pattern of relationship to his or her mother.
    b. The patient's level of ego functioning.
    c. The patient's intrapsychic structure.

127. Ms. M's early childhood behavior of lying across her mother's bed and breathing in rhythm with her mother's breathing is most likely an example of:

    a. Borderline clinging.
    b. Narcissistic mirroring.
    c. Narcissistic fusion.

128. What symptom is NOT indicative of the emergence of the effects of early trauma as personality is resolved?

    a. Persistent nightmares.
    b. Aversive behavior.
    c. Ease in talking about the trauma.
    d. Repetitive symbolic behavior.

129. Despite the very different outward appearances of patients with Exhibitionistic and Closet Narcissistic Personality Disorders, in making a differential diagnosis, where will you find similarities?

    a. In their intrapsychic structures.
    b. In their relationships with significant others.
    c. In their responses to the therapist.
    d. In the therapist's countertransference.

130. Ms. B states, "I'm looking for a therapist who will take care of me and not charge me for therapy." The therapist begins to feel guilty when insisting that she pay for her therapy. This is an example of:

    a. Narcissistic fusion of a grandiose self with the omnipotent other.
    b. A Schizoid individual seeking a safe but distant connection with a therapist.
    c. The therapist's resonating with a withdrawing object relations unit of the Borderline.
    d. The therapist's need to seek consultation on how to provide genetic interpretations with this resistance.

131. The function of the preorbital frontal cortex is:

    a.   To regulate affect and social emotional functioning.

    b.   To regulate cognitive functioning.

    c.   To regulate body functioning.

    d.   To integrate cognitive and affective input.

132. Confrontation is the therapeutic intervention utilized in the Masterson Approach with the Borderline Patient. Confrontation is defined as:

    a.   Aggressive undoing of maladaptive defenses to avoid further self-destructive actions.

    b.   A combination of interpretation and clarification to address maladaptive defenses and bring both sides of the split into the room.

    c.   Addressing the primitive defenses of splitting, avoidance, and denial by empathetically bringing the patient face to face with the maladaptive functioning of these defenses. It brings both sides of the split into the room.

133. The intrapsychic structure of a Schizoid Personality Disorder consists of:

    a.   A rewarding object relations unit and a sadistic object relations unit.

    b.   A sadistic object and a master self.

    c.   Two split object relations units.

134. The four functions of projective identification exclude which of the following?

    a.   Connect.

    b.   Communicate.

    c.   Control.

    d.   Contain.

    e.   Collude.

135. The interaction of the "behavioral" and "narrative" memory systems resolves traumatic experience by:

    a.   Synthesizing the verbal with the nonverbal.

    b.   Diminishing the anxiety level of the trauma.

    c.   Improving impulse control.

136. Bowlby's basic hypothetical assumption was:

    a. The achievement of attachment is purely biological.

    b. The child has an instinct for attachment, but was born without an attachment to the mother and had to establish one.

    c. The child has to separate from a symbiotic relationship with the mother.

    d. The child is prewired to see the mother as separate.

137. The most important reason for formulating a differential diagnosis is:

    a. It informs the therapist about the patient's symptoms.

    b. It is a guide to the kind of therapeutic interventions that will best serve the patient.

    c. It clarifies the patient's developmental issues and object relations.

138. A therapist has been working with a Disorder of the Self patient with Post-traumatic Stress Disorder for three years. The patient for the first time "feels," or takes in, the therapist's empathic acceptance of her, and the next day feels depression and suicidal despair. How could this be understood?

    a. The patient is defensively regressing as a way to get more attention.

    b. The experience of therapeutic attachment triggers the patient's abandonment depression.

    c. It is impossible to determine the reason for this without a differential diagnosis.

    d. None of the above.

139. During the testing phase, a Schizoid patient may remain quite withdrawn and silent, and insist that he or she "feels nothing here." The patient is testing to see if the therapist:

    a. Will become hostile and attacking.

    b. Will withdraw and withhold.

    c. Will tell him or her what he or she is thinking.

    d. All of the above.

140. Schizoid patients sometimes assert, well into the therapy, that they feel no connection to the therapist. The therapist should view this as:

    a. A sign that the therapy is going poorly.
    b. An example of defensive withdrawal.
    c. The patient's awareness of his or her actual deficits.
    d. The patient's self-activation.

141. Freud theorized that traumatic childhood experiences resulted in "strangulated affects" that could be released when:

    a. Interpreted from dreams.
    b. Resolved through the transference.
    c. Put into words.
    d. The perpetrator of the trauma is confronted.

142. The stages of therapy are:

    a. Testing, working through, and termination.
    b. Transference acting out, transference, and working through.
    c. Denial, anger, grief, and acceptance.

143. If a therapist interprets a Schizoid patient's behavior by telling the patient what he or she is feeling, the patient is likely to:

    a. Feel appropriated by the therapist.
    b. Feel much safer.
    c. Feel closer to the therapist.
    d. None of the above.

144. "What's on center stage?" refers to:

    a. Current Broadway productions.
    b. What the patient is presenting in the moment.
    c. What the therapist is experiencing in the moment.
    d. What both client and therapist are experiencing in the moment.

145. Mahler's stages of development were:

    a. Autism, symbiosis, separation–individuation.
    b. Secure and insecure.
    c. Oral, anal, phallic.
    d. Precognitive, cognitive.

146. When the therapist steps into the rewarding unit, the Borderline patient feels good, but the therapeutic work stops and becomes unproductive. As a result, the patient is likely to:

    a. Behave as regressed in the session.
    b. Act out outside of the session.
    c. Avoid any activation.
    d. All of the above.

147. It is important for the therapist to confront the patient when:

    a. The patient is in defense.
    b. The patient is focusing on himself or herself.
    c. The patient is expressing affect.
    d. The therapist disagrees with the patient's view of others.

148. Ms. B, a 50-year-old woman, enters therapy with you. She indicates that she had been in treatment 20 years earlier when her mother died. At that time, she had been diagnosed as Bipolar and was given lithium because she had been acting out by going to bars and sleeping with men, but then became very depressed. She took the drug, but said that it "only made me sick," so she stopped it after a 10-day period. Several months later, she stopped seeing the therapist and "got better by plunging myself into work." She no longer suffered the same symptoms. Her presenting problem this time was inappropriate outbursts of anger at her job and feelings of paralysis and depression when she was home alone on weekends. These feelings had begun after the departure of her female boss, with whom she had formed a very close, if at times stormy, relationship. In assessing this information, the most likely conclusion is that:

    a. The patient's difficulties stem from an untreated abandonment depression.
    b. The patient has had a recurrence of her Bipolar Disorder.
    c. The patient has an Impulse Disorder.

149. Transference acting out can best be described as a reenactment in the treatment of the patient's:

    a. Internalized object relations.
    b. Defenses.
    c. Response to intervention.

150. A therapist often needed to reschedule sessions in his busy practice, and found himself always asking one Schizoid patient to move her session. This therapist is:

    a. Resonating with the patient's master–slave unit.
    b. Acting out countertransference.
    c. Abandoning therapeutic neutrality.
    d. All of the above.

151. The "narrative" memory system:

    a. Translates traumatic experience into behavior.
    b. Understands traumatic experience without words.
    c. Holds traumatic experience in sensual impressions.
    d. Finds verbal expression for traumatic experience.

152. Masterson pinpoints the origins of the Borderline Personality Disorder as a developmental arrest in Margaret Mahler's:

    a. Rapprochement subphase.
    b. Symbiotic subphase.
    c. Practicing subphase.

153. A new patient with a Borderline diagnosis begins treatment with you and has three problems: (1) external functioning (poor boundaries with family and unemployed); (2) the need for you to be more caring and nurturing as a therapist; and (3) a history of childhood sexual abuse. Which problem should be the first area of therapeutic focus?

    a. External functioning.
    b. Ways to improve the therapist's level of caring.
    c. Childhood sexual abuse.
    d. All three should be treated at once.

154. A therapeutic alliance has been established with a Schizoid patient when the patient begins:

- a.   Attending sessions regularly, without missing.
- b.   Discussing other people in his or her life.
- c.   Consistently discussing his or her Schizoid dilemma.
- d.   Consistently acknowledging that he or she does not really want to come to sessions.

155. Ms. M was able to utilize therapy to manage career issues. She decided to take the LSATs with the intent of applying to law school. After she received her scores, which were very high, she procrastinated about sending out her applications. This is an example of:

- a.   The RORU.
- b.   The Disorder of the Self Triad.
- c.   Acting out the affects of abandonment depression.

156. Some of the capacities of the real self are:

- a.   Self-activation and assertion.
- b.   Entitlement and protection.
- c.   Object and emotional control.

157. Which of the Disorders of the Self is more likely to use trauma to justify regressing?

- a.   Borderline.
- b.   Schizoid.
- c.   Narcissistic.
- d.   Psychopathic.

158. It is important in treating a Schizoid patient to interpret the Schizoid dilemma:

- a.   In the patient's relations with coworkers.
- b.   In the patient's relations with the therapist.
- c.   In the patient's relations with his or her spouse.
- d.   In all aspects of the patient's life.

159. The abandonment depression of Schizoid individuals is particularly tinged with:

    a. Shame and humiliation.
    b. Profound aloneness and despair.
    c. Guilt and helplessness.
    d. Boredom and numbness.

160. Analytic neutrality means that the therapist is:

    a. Nondirective.
    b. Non-caretaking.
    c. Attentive to the frame.
    d. All of the above.

161. In doing trauma work with a patient with a Disorder of the Self, one of the primary goals is:

    a. To promote therapeutic safety by helping the patient to manage his or her annihilation anxiety.
    b. To track the number of defenses the particular Self Disorder employs and to respond appropriately.
    c. To process the countertransference dyadic interactions.
    d. To consolidate the testing phase of therapy.

162. A Schizoid patient consistently attended sessions, yet rarely said anything during the sessions. This most likely is an example of:

    a. Schizoid compromise.
    b. Schizoid despair.
    c. Schizoid emptiness.
    d. The therapist's acting out of the master role.

Answers

1. b (Chapter 3)
2. c (Chapter 6)
3. c (Chapter 9)
4. a (Chapter 8)
5. c (Chapter 8)
6. b (Chapter 9)
7. a, b, c (Chapter 3)
8. d (Chapter 9)
9. b (Chapter 8)

10. b (Chapter 5)
11. c (Chapter 4)
12. b (Chapter 4)
13. a (Chapter 9)
14. b (Chapter 7)
15. c (Chapter 3)
16. d (Chapter 6)
17. c (Chapter 2)
18. a (Chapter 5)
19. b (Chapter 5)

20. b (Chapter 3)
21. c (Chapter 7)
22. d (Chapter 6)
23. a (Chapter 9)
24. c (Chapter 2)
25. a (Chapter 5)
26. d (Chapter 5)

27. c (Chapter 4)
28. c (Chapter 6)
29. a (Chapter 8)

30. c (Chapter 2)
31. c (Chapter 5)
32. b (Chapter 8)
33. c (Chapter 5)
34. c (Chapter 6)
35. b, e (Chapter 8)
36. d (Chapter 5)
37. b (Chapter 6)
38. a (Chapter 9)
39. a (Chapter 7)

40. b (Chapter 6)
41. d (Chapter 9)
42. b (Chapter 8)
43. c, d (Chapter 2)
44. c (Chapter 5)
45. c (Chapter 6)
46. b (Chapter 6)
47. c (Chapter 3)
48. b (Chapter 3)
49. a (Chapter 5)

50. d (Chapter 6)
51. c, d (Chapter 8)

52.	c (Chapter 5)		90.	b (Chapter 7)
53.	c (Chapter 5)		91.	b (Chapter 6)
54.	c (Chapter 6)		92.	c (Chapter 8)
55.	c (Chapter 8)		93.	c (Chapter 2)
56.	a (Chapter 5)		94.	b (Chapter 2)
57.	d (Chapter 9)		95.	c (Chapter 4)
58.	a (Chapter 9)		96.	d (Chapter 9)
59.	a, d (Chapter 2)		97.	b (Chapter 3)
			98.	b (Chapter 6)
60.	d (Chapter 3)		99.	b (Chapter 9)
61.	f (Chapter 5)			
62.	d (Chapter 7)		100.	c (Chapter 8)
63.	b (Chapter 7)		101.	d (Chapter 6)
64.	d (Chapter 3)		102.	a (Chapter 2)
65.	b (Chapter 5)		103.	a (Chapter 5)
66.	d (Chapter 2)		104.	b (Chapter 8)
67.	a (Chapter 2)		105.	b (Chapter 3)
68.	d (Chapter 6)		106.	c (Chapter 8)
69.	c (Chapter 7)		107.	c (Chapter 6)
			108.	b (Chapter 2)
70.	c (Chapter 3)		109.	d (Chapter 2)
71.	b (Chapter 3)			
72.	a (Chapter 6)		110.	c (Chapter 4)
73.	d (Chapter 9)		111.	c (Chapter 3)
74.	b (Chapter 8)		112.	c (Chapter 9)
75.	d (Chapter 5)		113.	a, d (Chapter 2)
76.	d (Chapter 5)		114.	a (Chapter 4)
77.	d (Chapter 5)		115.	b (Chapter 2)
78.	a (Chapter 3)		116.	b (Chapter 7)
79.	b (Chapter 8)		117.	c (Chapter 7)
			118.	b (Chapter 2)
80.	a (Chapter 6)		119.	b (Chapter 6)
81.	a (Chapter 3)			
82.	d (Chapter 5)		120.	c (Chapter 6)
83.	a (Chapter 6)		121.	d (Chapter 7)
84.	c (Chapter 9)		122.	d (Chapter 7)
85.	c (Chapter 8)		123.	b (Chapter 7)
86.	d (Chapter 2)		124.	a (Chapter 3)
87.	c (Chapter 2)		125.	a, d (Chapter 2)
88.	a (Chapter 3)		126.	c (Chapter 4)
89.	c (Chapter 6)		127.	c (Chapter 6)

128. c (Chapter 8)
129. a (Chapter 6)

130. c (Chapter 9)
131. a (Chapter 2)
132. c (Chapter 5)
133. c (Chapter 7)
134. e (Chapter 9)
135. a (Chapter 8)
136. b (Chapter 2)
137. b (Chapter 4)
138. b (Chapter 9)
139. d (Chapter 7)

140. b (Chapter 7)
141. c (Chapter 8)
142. a (Chapter 3)
143. a (Chapter 7)
144. b (Chapter 3)
145. a (Chapter 2)

146. d (Chapter 5)
147. a (Chapter 5)
148. a (Chapter 4)
149. a (Chapter 4)

150. d (Chapter 7)
151. d (Chapter 8)
152. a (Chapter 5)
153. a (Chapter 9)
154. c (Chapter 7)
155. c (Chapter 5)
156. a (Chapter 3)
157. a (Chapter 9)
158. d (Chapter 7)
159. b (Chapter 7)

160. d (Chapter 3)
161. a (Chapter 9)
162. a (Chapter 7)

Bibliography

Adler, G. (1985). *Borderline Psychopathology and Its Treatment*. New York: Jason Aronson.

Ainsworth, M. D. S., Blehar, M., Waters, E., & Wall, S. (1978). *Patterns of Attachment: A Psychological Study of the Strange Situation*. Hillsdale, NJ: Erlbaum.

Akhtar, S. (1987). Schizoid personality disorder: A synthesis of developmental dynamic, and descriptive features. *American Journal of Psychotherapy, 41*, 499–518.

Bernstein, D., Cohen, P., Skodol, A., Bezirganian, S., & Brook, J. (1996). Childhood antecedents of adolescent personality disorders. *American Journal of Psychiatry*, July, 153–157.

Blos, P. (1962). *On Adolescence*. New York: Free Press.

Bowlby, J. (1969). *Attachment and Loss:* Vol. 1, *Attachment*. (1973); Vol. 2, *Separation: Anxiety and Anger*. (1980); Vol. 3, *Loss: Sadness and Depression*. New York: Basic Books.

Bowlby, J. (1988). *Secure Base: Parent–Child Attachment and Healthy Human Development*. New York: Basic Books.

Brazelton, T. B. (1980). New knowledge about the infant from current research: Implications for psychoanalysis. Presented at the American Psychoanalytic Association meeting, San Francisco, CA, May.

Breuer, J., & Freud, S. (1895/1955). *Studies on Hysteria* (J. Strachey, Ed. & Trans.). New York: Basic Books.

Brown, D., Scheflin, A. W., & Hammond, D. C. (1988). *Memory, Trauma Treatment, and the Law*. New York: Norton.

Carlson, V., Cicchetti, D., Barnett, D., & Braunwald, K. G. (1989). Finding order in disorganization: Lessons from research on maltreated infants' attachments to their caregivers (pp. 494–526). In D. Cicchetti & V. Carlson (Eds.), *Child Maltreatment: Theory and Research on the Causes and Consequences of Maltreatment*. New York: Cambridge University Press.

Diagnostic and Statistical Manual of Mental Disorders (4th ed., 1994). Washington, DC: American Psychiatric Association.

Emde, R. N., & Sorce, J. E. (1983). The rewards of infancy: Emotional availability and maternal referencing. In J. D. Call, E. Galenson, & R. Tyson (Eds.), *Frontiers in Infant Psychiatry*, Vol. 2. New York: Basic Books.

Erickson, M., Sroufe, L. A., & Egeland, B. (1985). The relationship between quality of attachment and behavior problems in preschool in a high-risk sample (pp. 147–166). In I. Bretherton & E. Waters (Eds.), *Growing Points of Attachment Theory and Research*, Monographs of the Society for Research in Child Development, 50 (1–2, Serial No. 209).

Erikson, E. H. (1956). The problem of ego identity. *Journal of the American Psychoanalytic Association*, 4, 56–121.

Fairbairn, W. R. D. (1984). *Psychoanalytic Studies of the Personality*. London: Routledge & Kegan Paul.

Fisher, R. (1989). Countertransference to transference acting out of a Narcissistic Personality Disorder. In J. F. Masterson & R. Klein (Eds.), *Psychotherapy of the Disorders of the Self*. New York: Brunner/Mazel.

Fonagy, P. (2001). *Attachment Theory and Psychoanalysis*. New York: Other Press.

Freud, A. (1958). Adolescence (pp. 255–278). In *Psychoanalytic Study of the Child* (Vol. 12). New York: International Universities Press.

Freud, S. (1953). Further recommendations in the techniques of psychoanalysis: Recollection, repetition and working through (pp. 366–376). In *Collected Papers*, Vol. II. London: Hogarth.

Freud, S. (1957/1914). On narcissism: An introduction. In *Standard Edition*. London: Hogarth.

Gabbard, G. O., et al. (1996). *The Borderline Personality Disorder: Tailoring the Psychotherapy to the Patient*. Washington, DC: American Psychiatric Press.

Greenacre, P. (1960). Regression and fixation. In *Journal of the American Psychoanalytic Association*, 8, 703–723.

Gunderson, J. (1996). The Borderline patient's intolerance of aloneness, insecure attachments and therapist's availability. *American Journal of Psychiatry*, June.

Gunderson, J. G., & Zanarim, M. C. (1989). Pathogenesis of borderline personality (pp. 25–48). In A. Tasman, R. E. Hales, & A. J. Frances, *American Psychiatric Press Review of Psychiatry*, Vol. 8. Washington, DC: American Psychiatric Press.

Guntrip, H. (1969). *Schizoid Phenomena, Object Relations and the Self*. New York: International Universities Press.

Hall, J. (1985). Idealizing transference: Disruptions and repairs in progress. In A. Goldberg (Ed.), *Self Psychology*, Vol. 1. New York: Guilford.

Heinicke, C., & Westheimer, I. (1966). *Brief Separations*. New York: International Universities Press; London: Longmans Green.

Kernberg, O. F. (1967). Borderline personality organization. *Journal of the American Psychoanalytic Association*, *15*, 641–685.

Kernberg, O. F. (1968). Treatment of patients with Borderline personality organization. *International Journal of Psychoanalysis*, *49*, 600–619.

Kernberg, O. F. (1974a). Contrasting viewpoints regarding the nature and psychoanalytic treatment of Narcissistic personalities: A preliminary communication. *Journal of the American Psychoanalytic Association*, *22*, 255–267.

Kernberg, O. F. (1974b). Further considerations of the treatment of Narcissistic personalities. *International Journal of Psychoanalysis*, *55*, 215–240.

Kernberg, O. (1975). *Borderline Conditions and Pathological Narcissism*. New York: Jason Aronson.

Klein, M. (1946). Notes on some Schizoid mechanisms. In J. Riviere (Ed.), *Developments in Psychoanalysis*. London: Hogarth.

Klein, R. (1989). Diagnosis and treatment of the lower-level Borderline patient. In J. F. Masterson & R. Klein (Eds.), *Psychotherapy of the Disorders of the Self*. New York: Brunner/Mazel.

Klein, R. (1993). Schizoid personality disorder. In J. F. Masterson, *The Emerging Self*. New York: Brunner/Mazel.

Klein, R. (1995). Schizoid disorders of the self. In J. F. Masterson, & R. Klein (Eds.), *Disorders of the Self: New Therapeutic Horizons — The Masterson Approach*. New York: Brunner/ Mazel.

Kohut, H. (1966). Forms and transformations of narcissism. *Journal of the American Psychoanalytic Association*, *14*, 243–272.

Kohut, H. (1968). Psychoanalytic treatment of Narcissistic Personality Disorder: Outline of a systematic approach. *Psychoanalytic Study of the Child*, *23*, 86–113.

Kohut, H. (1969). Panel on Narcissistic resistance (N. Regal, Reporter). *Journal of the American Psychoanalytic Association*, *17*, 941–954.

Kohut, H. (1971). *The Analysis of the Self: A Systematic Approach to the Psychoanalytic Treatment of Narcissistic Personality Disorders*. New York: International Universities Press.

Kohut, H. (1977). *The Restoration of the Self*. New York: International Universities Press.

Kohut, H. (1987). Narcissism as a resistance and as a driving force in psychoanalysis. In D. Millman, & G. Goldman (Eds.), *Techniques of Working with Resistance*. New Jersey: Jason Aronson.

Linehan, M. M. (1996). Dialectical behavior therapy (DBT) for Borderline Personality Disorder. *Journal of California Alliance for the Mentally Ill*, *8*(1), 44–46.

Lyons-Ruth, K. (1989). From birth to five: Development pathways of the young child at social risk. Address to the Bunting Institute Colloquium Series, Radcliffe College, Cambridge, MA, February.

Lyons-Ruth, K. (1991). Rapprochement or approchement: Mahler's theory reconsidered from the vantage point of recent research on early attachment relationships. *Psychoanalytic Psychology, 8*(1), 1–23.

Lyons-Ruth, K., Connell, D. B., Grunebaum, H., & Botein, S. (1990). Infants at social risk: Maternal depression and family support services as mediators in infant development and security of attachment. *Child Development, 61*, 85–98.

MacKinnon, R., & Michaels, R. (1971). *The Psychiatric Interview*. Philadelphia: Saunders.

Mahler, M. S. (1968). *On Human Symbiosis and the Vicissitudes of Individuation*. New York: International Universities Press.

Mahler, M. S. (1968). *On Human Symbiosis and the Vicissitudes of Individuation*, Vol. 1, *Infantile Psychosis*. New York: International Universities Press.

Mahler, M. S. (1972a). On the first three subphases of the separation–individuation process. *International Journal of Psychoanalysis, 53*, 333–338.

Mahler, M. S. (1972b). Rapprochement subphase of the separation–individuation process. *Psychoanalytic Quarterly, 41*, 487–506.

Mahler, M. S., & Kaplan, L. (1977). Developmental aspects in the assessment of Narcissistic and so-called Borderline personalities. In P. Hartocollis (Ed.), *Borderline Personality Disorders: The Concept, the Syndrome, the Patient*. New York: International Universities Press.

Mahler, M. S., Pine, F., & Bergman A. (1975). *The Psychological Birth of the Human Infant*. New York: Basic Books.

Main, M., & Hesse, E. (1990). Parents' unresolved traumatic experiences are related to infant disorganized status: Is frightened and/or frightening parental behavior the linking mechanism? (pp. 161–184). In M. Greenberg, D. Cicchetti, & E. M. Cummings (Eds.), *Attachment in the Preschool Years: Theory, Research and Intervention*. Chicago: University of Chicago Press.

Main, M., & Solomon, J. (1990). Procedures for identifying infants as disorganized/disoriented during the Ainsworth strange situation (pp. 121–160). In M. Greenberg, D. Cicchetti, & E. M. Cummings (Eds.), *Attachment in the Preschool Years: Theory, Research and Intervention*. Chicago: University of Chicago Press.

Masterson, J. F. (1967). *The Psychiatric Dilemma of Adolescence*. Boston: Little Brown.

Masterson, J. F. (1972). *Treatment of the Borderline Adolescent: A Developmental Approach*. New York: Wiley.

Masterson, J. F. (1976). *The Psychotherapy of the Borderline Adult: A Developmental Approach*. New York: Brunner/Mazel.

Masterson, J. F. (1980). *From Borderline Adolescent to Functioning Adult: The Test of Time*. New York: Brunner/Mazel.

Masterson, J. F. (1981). *The Narcissistic and Borderline Disorders: An Integrated Developmental Approach*. New York: Brunner/Mazel.

Masterson, J. F. (1983). *Countertransference and Psychotherapeutic Technique: Teaching Seminars on the Psychotherapy of the Borderline Adult.* New York: Brunner/Mazel.

Masterson, J. F. (1985). *The Real Self: A Developmental Self and Object Relations Approach.* New York: Brunner/Mazel.

Masterson, J. F. (1988). *The Search for the Real Self: Unmasking the Personality Disorders of Our Age.* New York: Free Press.

Masterson, J. F. (1993). *The Emerging Self: A Developmental, Self, and Object Relations Approach to the Treatment of the Closet Narcissistic Disorder of the Self.* New York: Brunner/Mazel.

Masterson, J. F. (2000). *The Personality Disorders: A New Look at the Developmental Self and Object Relations Approach.* Phoenix: Zeig, Tucker.

Masterson, J. F., & Klein, R. (Eds.). (1989). *Psychotherapy of the Disorders of the Self: The Masterson Approach.* New York: Brunner/Mazel.

Masterson, J. F., & Klein, R. (Eds.). (1995). *Disorders of the Self: New Therapeutic Horizons.* New York: Brunner/Mazel.

Masterson, J. F., Tolpin, M., & Sifneos, P. E. (1991). *Comparing Psychoanalytic Psychotherapies: Developmental, Self and Object Relations, Self Psychology and Short-Term Dynamic.* New York: Brunner/Mazel.

Meissner, W. W. (1984). *The Borderline Spectrum, Differential Diagnosis and Developmental Issues.* New York: Jason Aronson.

Miller, A. (1979). *Prisoners of Childhood.* New York: Basic Books.

Moskowitz, M., Monk, C., Kaye, C., & Ellman, S. (Eds.). (1997). *The Neurological and Developmental Basis for Psychotherapeutic Intervention.* New Jersey: Jason Aronson.

Orcutt, C. (1995). The influence of early trauma on the developing self. In J. F. Masterson & R. Klein (Eds.), *Disorders of the Self: New Therapeutic Horizons.* New York: Brunner/Mazel.

Orcutt, C. (1995). Uncovering "forgotten" child abuse in the psychotherapy of a Borderline Disorder of the Self. In J. F. Masterson & R. Klein (Eds.), *Disorders of the Self: New Therapeutic Horizons.* New York: Brunner/Mazel.

Orcutt, C. (1995). Integration of Multiple Personality Disorder in the context of the Masterson Approach. In J. F. Masterson & R. Klein (Eds.), *Disorders of the Self: New Therapeutic Horizons.* New York: Brunner/Mazel.

Racker, H. (1968). *Transference and Countertransference.* New York: International Universities Press.

Reid, W. H. (Ed.). (1978). *The Psychopath: A Comprehensive Study of the Antisocial Disorders and Behaviors.* New York: Brunner/Mazel.

Rinsley, D. B., & Hale, D. D. (1962). Psychiatric hospital treatment of adolescents. *Archives of General Psychiatry, 7,* 207–294.

Robertson, J. (1953). Some responses of young children to loss of maternal care. *Nursing Times, 49,* 382–386.

Sanders, L. W. (1969). The longitudinal course of early mother–child interaction: Cross-case comparison in a sample of mother–child pairs. In B. M. Foss (Ed.), *Determinants of Infant Behavior*, Vol. 4. London and New York: Barnes & Noble.

Schore, A. N. (1994). *Affect Regulation and the Origin of the Self*. Hillsdale, NJ: Erlbaum.

Seinfeld, J. (1991). *The Empty Core: An Object Relations Approach to Psychotherapy of the Schizoid Personality*. New York: Jason Aronson.

Shapiro, D. (1965). *Neurotic Styles*. New York: Basic Books.

Siegel, D. (1999). *The Developing Mind*. New York and London: Guilford.

Spitz, R. A. (1965). *The First Year of Life*. New York: International Universities Press.

Sroufe, L. A., Carlson, E. A., Levy, A. K., & Egeland, B. (1999). *Development and Psychopathology* (pp. 1–13). London: Cambridge University Press.

Stern, D. N. (1985). *The Interpersonal World of the Infant — A View From Psychoanalysis and Developmental Psychology*. New York: Basic Books.

Thomas, A., Chess, S., & Birch, H. (1968). *Temperament and Behavior Disorders in Children*. New York: New York University Press.

Van der Kolk, B. A., McFarlane, A. C., & Weisaeth, L. (Eds.). (1996). *Traumatic Stress*. New York: Guilford.

Winnicott, D. (1965). *Maturation Process and the Facilitating Environment*. New York: International Universities Press.

Index

Testing phase of therapy, 33, 87
Therapeutic alliance, 33, 66, 70, 83, 84, 87, 101, 102, 171
Therapeutic neutrality, 31, 66, 82–83, 123
Transference, 30–32, 38–39, 52–53, 65–66, 83, 84, 85, 87, 105, 108, 138, 170
Trauma, 111–118, 123, 141, 148, 155, 165, 172

Winnicott, D., 14
Withdrawing object relations part unit (WORU), 28, 41, 61, 63, 66, 68, 69, 147, 151, 153